Freedom through Surrender:

A 31-Day Devotional

By Jason West

Endorsements

"Jason West has written a book that is divinely inspired that reminds us as Christians that love is the most powerful tool that we have on this Christian journey. It will allow us to overcome fear. It will allow us to have the faith necessary to trust God's character when we have doubts or don't understand. It will allow us to acknowledge Him in all our ways and lean not to our own understanding. Jason reminds us of the power of prayer in all circumstances and God's faithfulness in answering our prayers, and gives the assurance that ultimately we can let go and let God be God not matter what. This book can change your life and your most important relationship: your relationship with God."

John W. Ewing, Jr

Douglas County Treasurer

Associate Minister Salem Baptist Church

"*Freedom through Surrender* is the heart of this devotional book by Jason West. Jason, in using his own life's experiences, brings practical insight, gives encouragement and allows the reader an opportunity to surrender their daily walk to the Lord."

Zoie Hicks Kern

Gatekeeper and Administrative Assistant to Governor Sam Brownback

"Jason has created an inspiring devotional book with life lessons for all to apply. It comes with the freshness of youth coupled with the wisdom of God's Word. Read it and be blessed."

Dr. Alan Langstaff

President, Kairos Ministries

"Jason West possesses an amazingly mature understanding of the Christian life. This book is your guide to knowing and experiencing the Lord more intimately. So, I suggest rather than thirty days, you consider going through it at least three times (90 days). You will rise to a new level of spiritual life and understanding. Thank you, Jason, for this remarkable gift!"

Eddie Smith

Co-founder and executive director of the U.S. Prayer Center, in Houston, Texas

Owner/CEO, Worldwide Publishing Group, LLC

© 2019 by Jason B. West

Anointed 2 Go MdM

Bellevue, NE

All rights reserved. This book is protected by the copyright laws of the United States of America. This book or any parts therein may not be reproduced, distributed, copied or transmitted in any form, not electronic, mechanical or any other means, or stored in a database or retrieval system without the prior written permission of the publisher. The use of short quotations or occasional passage copying for personal or group study is permitted and encouraged.

Unless otherwise identified, all Scripture quotations are from the New King James Version. Copyright © 1982 by Thomas Nelson, Inc. Used by permission. All rights reserved.

Scripture quotations identified (AMP) or "The Amplified Bible" are taken from THE AMPLIFIED BIBLE. Old Testament copyright © 1965, 1987 by The Zondervan Corporation. The Amplified New Testament copyright © 1958, 1987 by The Lockman Foundation. Used by permission.

Scripture quotations identified KJV are from the King James Version of the Bible.

Scripture quotations identified (MSG) or "The Message Bible" are taken from THE MESSAGE. Copyright © 1993, 1994, 1995, 1996, 2000, 2001, 2002. Used by permission of NavPress Publishing Group.

Scripture quotations identified (NIV) or "New International Version" are taken from the HOLY BIBLE, NEW INTERNATIONAL VERSION®. Copyright 1973, 1978, 1984 by International Bible Society. Used by permission of Zondervan. All rights reserved.

Paperback: 978-1-68411-686-7

Hardcover: 978-0-359-32784-3

For further information, to contact Jason West for speaking, or to order resources:

Please email runningfree@cox.net or go to http://kingdomexpressions.wordpress.com.

Dedication

    I dedicate this book to the One Who is the reason I write, the reason I sing, the reason I teach, and the reason I live. God, my Everlasting Father, my Lord Jesus, and the Holy Spirit who lives inside me—without You I have no purpose, no meaning, and no reason to live. Because of You I am complete, whole, and lacking nothing. Thank You for being my All-In-All. Thank You for Your faithfulness and love for me. Thank You for saving me and setting me free from my sins, my shame, and my sorrow. You alone deserve my worship, adoration, and affection.

    To God be the glory.

Acknowledgments

The process of writing a book is such a collaborative effort that many people's names should really be on the front cover because each one played a part. Thank you to every person who helped with this process, whether through specific tasks or overall encouragement.

Thank you, Mom and Dad, for your continued encouragement through this journey. Thank you also Dad for writing the foreword and for completing the second edit for the book. I appreciated all your thoughts and input!

Thank you, Gary Peterson, for completing the first edit and review of the book. Your insights and comments were invaluable!

Thank you, Bill Vincent and the team from Revival Waves of Glory Publishing, for working with me to complete the formatting, cover design, and publication of this book!

Thank you to John Ewing, Zoie Kern, Alan Langstaff, and Eddie Smith for taking the time to read this manuscript and offer your endorsements. I greatly appreciate it!

Thank you to my students, who inspired a number of topics, anecdotes, and examples throughout the book. The inspiration for a number of these devotion entries stemmed from discussions and topics we covered in class—memories I will definitely treasure.

Thank you to my church family at Kingdom Encounters for encouraging me to write, praying for me, and always speaking words of life over me! Fresh oil!

Thank you to my friends, family, and mentors who have poured into me over the years. It is through receiving exhortations from people like you that helps keep me motivated and driven to seek the Lord with all my heart.

Thank you, God, for planting this desire in my heart, giving me the ideas and topics to write, and sustaining me with the grace needed to complete it. I am eternally grateful for the great things You have done.

Contents

Endorsements 3
Dedication 7
Acknowledgments 9
Foreword By Pastor Jay West 13
Introduction (Read This First!) 17
A Heartfelt Prayer 19
Section I: It All Comes Down to Love 21
Day 1: What Does Love Look Like? 23
Day 2: There Is No Fear in Love 27
Day 3: Thoughts on Fear and Love 31
Day 4: Never Have I Seen the Righteous Forsaken ... 37
Section II: Got Faith? 39
Day 5: Unanswered Questions 41
Day 6: Trust His Character 43
Day 7: Where's Your Faith? 47
Day 8: Have Faith, My Friends 49
Day 9: F A I T H | R I S K 53
Day 10: Miracles 57
Section III: The Battle on Our Knees 61
Day 11 Prayer—The Long and Short of It 63
Day 12: Less Talk—More Prayer 67
Day 13: Biblical Problem Solving 69
Day 14: The Battle 71
Day 15: Find Your Aaron and Hur 75

Section IV: Learning (The Easy Way) 79
Day 16: The Learning Curve 81
Day 17: Figuring It Out 83
Day 18: Evidence 87

Section V: This One's for All the Control Freaks...
...... 91
Day 19: Eternity Calling 93
Day 20: Transform Us 95
Day 21: He Wants It All 99
Day 22: Lord *and* Savior 101
Day 23: Get Hungry 105
Day 24: The Pressure Is OFF: No More Striving 107
Day 25: The Praise of God 111
Day 26: My Life as a Game of Whac-A-Mole 115
Day 27: So, You Think You're Entitled? 119

Section VI: Can I Get a Witness? 121
Day 28: Only Light 123
Day 29: The Power of the Holy Spirit 125
Day 30: Take a Stand 129
Day 31: Compelled by Love 131
Appendix A: Do You Know Him? 135
Appendix B: Other Products Available from Anointed 2 Go MdM
...... 139
Appendix C Notes 143

Foreword
By Pastor Jay West

Freedom through Surrender is a catchy title because in our natural way of thinking, it almost sounds erroneous. Let me explain.

We have all seen enough TV shows and movies to know that when someone surrenders, it usually means that they give up their rights, current lifestyle, and often many freedoms. Examples of this include a criminal to the police, a platoon of soldiers to the enemy, or perhaps an individual surrendering his or her car to the bank due to an inability to pay the loan. All of these involve the loss of something valuable with the additional time of either being incarcerated, jailed, or at the very least put in a vulnerable position where life is harder than it was prior to the act of surrendering.

But with God, the outcome is entirely different. Through surrender and the process of giving up, new freedoms are discovered and revealed that most thought were not possible. Only through obedience and the act of surrender do we see Jesus moving in and through our circumstances to bring liberty, blessings, new growth through this fresh journey, and ultimately an outcome that most would not imagine was possible. We emerge on the other side transformed and revived, with a Holy Spirit-inspired refreshing that lasts a lifetime. There really is freedom through surrender.

Matthew 7:13-14 declares, "Enter by the narrow gate; for wide is the gate and broad is the way that leads to destruction, and there are many who go in by it. Because narrow is the gate and difficult is the way which leads to life, and there are few who find it."

In our present life we are confronted with these truths on a consistent basis, and we must look at our circumstances and lifecycles with biblical glasses rather than earthly tainted ones. Often the wide gate looks enticing, romancing, and intriguing because of the sheer number of people who are following that path. But on the other side the path narrows and the journey becomes containing, crowded, and confusing. It looked good at the beginning, but now it has become confining, and many find themselves struggling to even remain upright and breathing. Instead of times of refreshing coming from the Lord, it seems like we are gasping and grasping for something, anything, or anyone who can get us out of this mess.

The other option is this little narrow gate, with a path that is hard to distinguish, primarily because very few people are choosing it. In fact, it looks more like a crime scene with blood stains on the stepping stones. Few are walking this way because the appearance lacks the vitality and bold colors, the alluring party flavor, the fascinating atmosphere, and the attractive sounds that the other gate displays. As a result this gate is often overlooked and undervalued because surrendering to it seems like a waste of time and energy. Who wants to hang out where drops of blood are the ink that is used to encourage people to respond to this invitation?

If only they would know that total surrender to the narrow gate will bring them greater freedom than they have ever known and experienced. Had they only known that the other side of the gate reveals the greatest light they have ever seen, with the greatest of mobility to see incredible and amazing things accomplished that most might call a miracle, but those who surrender to it just refer to it as a day spent with Jesus. Surrendering to the Lord, brings a new awareness and new options for living that others never experience, encounter, or enjoy.

To participate in this surrender process you need only give up, give in, and give over to the blessing of knowing God. The freedom you will experience will ultimately change your life for the good and influence others to do the same.

I have known Jason all of his life. I have very few people I can literally say that about, and since he was very young, he has loved to worship God and pray to Him. He often surrenders his own schedule and other worldly pleasures to spend quality time with the Lord. Frequently as I am going to sleep, he is just entering into an extended time of prayer, soaking, and worship that is rarely seen in a 26-year-old.

Because of the anointing he carries, you will be challenged, inspired, challenged, blessed and challenged again and again to surrender parts of your life to Jesus. And while you can easily read this book in one month, I encourage you to read it for at least three months in a row, and journal your thoughts about each of the day's presentations that are contained in the book. Be open to how God may change your perspective about surrender as you go through the book a second and third time. Look for those golden moments when God speaks to you and brings clarity of vision, offering diversity in presentation while solidifying your strength in the faith that you currently walk in. The reality is that the more you surrender, the more you will experience freedom. The choice is yours. It just depends on how free you really want to be.

Introduction (Read This First!)

To the reader:

Thank you for taking the time to read my book. Whether you purchased it, received it as a gift, read it online, or just found it lying around somewhere and decided to pick it up, I pray that the Lord uses it to speak to you in mighty ways.

As you read, I want you to be aware of a few things. First, this book features different styles of writing. There is a variety of journal entries, expository essays, and even some poetry. The devotions were each written individually and at separate times throughout the past few years. Some are more formal; some are more personal. But all of them are attempts to share from my heart about things God has been showing me and the things I've been wrestling with and ruminating on throughout the past few years. I don't claim to have all the answers—but I pray that you will be edified and inspired and that, as you read, you will take these thoughts to the Lord for further revelation on the subjects brought forth.

Additionally, because the entries in this book were written at different times and in different styles over the past few years, it was not my intention for them to form a cohesive unit. But at the suggestion of a few people who read the entries along the way, I decided to compile them together into this devotional book. With that in mind, I have tried my best to categorize the entries into a few sections, connecting common themes and similar entries together.

Finally, this book is relatively short. While it may be tempting to sit down and read through the whole thing quickly, that really is not the intent. I believe that the best value can be gained from this book if you take your time and read one entry per day. I have divided the book into thirty-one devotional entries; thus, you could read one entry a day for a month. You can read the book however you see fit, of course; however, my encouragement to you is to take it slowly and enjoy the unfolding process.

Again, thank you for your time, attention, and thoughtful dedication as the reader. I pray the Lord ministers to you as much through this book as He did to me when I wrote the entries.

God's richest blessings to you,

Jason B. West

Kingdom Expressions Worship Leader

Kingdom Encounters, Omaha, NE

runningfree@cox.net

http://www.kingdomexpressions.wordpress.com

A Heartfelt Prayer

Father, we come to You this day, boldly asking You to do the miraculous in our midst. Lord, as Your disciples and apostles prayed, so we also pray the same: Increase our faith.[i] Forgive us for our low expectations. Create in us a hunger for You that won't be satisfied until we see the greater things You've promised. Let us not settle for second rate or second best when you invite us to sit with You and feast at the table. We want to see the greater things. We want to see revival. We ask for more.

Forgive us for being so wrapped up in our own little worlds that we failed to see the bigger picture of what You were doing around us. Teach us to open our eyes to see the wonderful things You are doing. Show us how to have a greater appreciation for the blessings You bestow. As the line of a powerful worship song says, we ask that You would "break [our] heart for what breaks Yours" and "show [us] how to love like You have loved [us]."[ii] Give us hearts of compassion for the lost, the hurting, and the broken. Grant us an enthusiasm and endurance that cannot be matched by the mere strivings of man but can only be bestowed by the one true eternal God.

Bring us to the well of life, that we may drink of the water that cleanses, purifies, and restores. Take us to Your fountain that springs forth with bursts of refreshing mists. Guide us to the altar, where we may humbly bow before You and humbly give You our hearts. Lead us to the cross, that we may die to ourselves and experience the resurrection power of our Savior. Compel us through Your Spirit, that we may walk by the Spirit and live by the Spirit all the days of our lives.

Create in us a passion for Your name unlike any passion we've ever had before. Show us how to give You everything. Show us how to seek after Your heart. Make us more like You, that we may bear Your light and life to all whom we encounter.

All these things we ask, trusting and believing in the mighty, matchless name of Jesus.

Section I:
It All Comes Down to Love

Day 1: What Does Love Look Like?

Love is patient[iii]

(Love is not always convenient)

Love is kind

(Particularly when you don't feel like being kind)

It does not envy

(Especially when you really want what someone else has)

It does not boast

(Even when you really crave attention and recognition)

It is not proud

(Love leads you to have a right understanding of who you are and Whose you are)

It does not dishonor others

(It values honor at all costs)

It is not self-seeking

(It takes self out of the equation and focuses entirely on others)

It is not easily angered

(It takes a lot to make you angry, but if you do get angry, it is because of injustice—for which your love compels you to action)

It keeps no record of wrongs

(Love's power is not weakened, no matter how many times the other person fails. It does not focus on the ninety-nine wrong things; it celebrates the one right thing. Love finds gold in the midst of dirt.)

Love does not delight in evil but rejoices with the truth

(Love without truth is not really love at all)

It always protects

(Even at the risk of making yourself look bad for the sake of protecting others)

Always trusts

(No matter how many times people may hurt you and make you feel like you can't trust anyone anymore)

Always hopes

(Even if every situation around you seems utterly hopeless)

Always perseveres

(True love may grow weary, but it never quits)

Love never fails

(There is nothing that can stop its power)

Day 2:
There Is No Fear in Love

"For our gospel did not come to you in word only, but also in power..."

~1 Thessalonians 1:5

"For the kingdom of God is not in word but in power."

~1 Corinthians 4:20

      A couple months ago, I had a very profound dream that I believe was inspired by the Holy Spirit. Here is the gist of it: I was sitting in a large arena at a conference, listening to a man speaking God's Word. The man was saying something to this effect: "So many people live in defeat and hopelessness when they were never supposed to live that way. God has unlimited spiritual riches in store for each one of you, but it breaks His heart when you deny Him the opportunity to bestow those things on you because you say, 'I'm unworthy' or 'I don't deserve this.' He is grieved when you deny Him the opportunity to pour everything out that He has in store! He just wants you to open your arms and receive."

In the dream, I was so deeply moved, that I began to cry out, "God, I just want all that You have for me!" It was very apparent in the dream that I was weeping. When I awoke, and for the rest of that day, I was deeply moved and kept thinking about that dream.

Then, a few weeks later, I traveled with some leaders from my church to a conference. On the first night of the conference during the worship music time, I experienced something that I've never experienced before: I began to cry uncontrollably. The presence of God in the room and in my heart was so strong at that moment that I was just overwhelmed by His goodness and love. I felt like I saw a tiny glimpse of heaven, and that tiny glimpse was enough to send me over the edge. I was deeply convicted that there is so much more to life than we can even comprehend, and there is so much more to God than we can ever imagine. As I cried, I remembered the dream I had had a few weeks prior, and this set me to crying even more. In a sense, I felt like I was living that dream in real life. So I spoke the words out loud that I said in the dream: "God, I just want all that You have for me!"

Through these experiences, I believe the Lord was revealing to me a profound truth that He desires that all His people would walk in and believe: He has created us to live in power. It grieves my heart when I see believers going through life with an attitude of defeat. It's like they expect things to go wrong before they even happen. They live their lives out of fear, and this fear imprisons them and keeps them bound in chains, not releasing them to the fullness of who God has called them to be. These people are afraid of getting sick; afraid of losing their job; afraid of running out of money; afraid of what people think of them; afraid of relational problems; afraid of the unknown; and afraid of the enemy and his attacks and schemes. They have the fear of man rather than the fear of God. I know, for I have lived in this place before.

Yet, what does the Word of God say about this? "There is no fear in love; but perfect love casts out fear, because fear involves torment" (1 John 4:18). Jesus is perfect love. Fear is the opposite of love. By opening the door to fear, we invite torment into our lives. Also, "God has not given us a spirit of fear, but of power and of love and of a sound mind" (2 Tim. 1:7). Fear is the antithesis of power. By these verses, we can be sure of this: Any kind of fear in our lives does not and cannot come from God. God's heart is to give us the remedy to fear: Walking in power, love, and a sound mind!

You see, fear brings a spirit of torment into our lives. And that spirit of torment limits us and inhibits us from doing what God has created us to do. We can't serve God the way we were created to serve Him when we are constantly walking in fear. Surely, it breaks God's heart when He sees His children walking around with their heads down, fearful of what might be around every corner. By living in this type of fear, what we are unintentionally saying is, "God, I don't trust You. My problems are bigger than You are. The enemy has more power than You do. I want to serve You, but I'm not really sure You will come through for me." As a child of God, if I walk in fear, I am being a poor representation of my Father. The more I live in fear, the less effective I am for the kingdom of God. Fear stops me from taking risks and getting out of my comfort zone when the Holy Spirit leads me to step out in faith.

The solution? Know who you are and Whose you are. The lyrics of two worship songs come to mind: "You're a good, good Father. It's Who You are….and I'm loved by You. It's who I am."[iv] Also, "I'm no longer a slave to fear. I am a child of God."[v] We need to live like we believe this. The key to living this way is walking in His power. And the key to walking in His power is inviting the Holy Spirit into every corner of our lives so that we would truly submit every part of our being to Him. He comes to take away our fears and replace them with a spirit of power, love, and a sound mind. As we invite Him to come and ask Him to pour out everything He has for us, we will see just how great and unlimited His riches in glory are.

Too many believers are living powerless lives because they do not realize the extent of power that God desires them to walk in every day. As the Scriptures at the top of this devotion say, the gospel (good news) of Jesus Christ is a gospel that is not in word alone but also in power! Words without power have no effect. It is only when we invite the power of the Holy Spirit into our lives to back up His Word that we truly experience freedom from fear and worry—freedom we were always created to walk in.

You are no longer a slave to fear, and you have a good, good Father. Live that way. And never hesitate to ask God to give you everything He has for you. That is not a selfish request; it is a humble request from a child who knows who his Father is. Most certainly, as He answers that request, you will live in greater freedom and power than you ever have before, and you will help others to do the same.

Day 3: Thoughts on Fear and Love

Whenever we feel afraid, it is a profound reminder of the frailty of humanity and the ill effects of sin in the world. No human who ever lived has been immune to feeling afraid at some point in his or her life. Because we live in a fallen world, our lives are filled with opportunities to be afraid. Sometimes our fears are very rational and lead us to make wise choices, such as choosing not to touch a hot stove out of fear of getting burned.

However, many times our fears are actually irrational and lead us to shy away from doing what we really were created to do. We don't say what we should because we're afraid of what others will think. We don't take risks because we're afraid of failure. We don't reach out to help someone because the last time we did that we became hurt in the process. These irrational fears cause us to wall ourselves off and do whatever it takes to avoid getting hurt. Yet, no matter how hard we try not to get hurt, it is impossible to completely protect ourselves from getting hurt in this life.

How do we deal with pain? Recently, I was listening to a message by Pastor Kris Vallotton, and one of the things he said in that message was that when we say, "I'll never let myself get hurt again," we're really saying, "I'll never love again."

I'll never love again.

Have those words ever entered your mind?

In order for love to be love, it cannot be rooted in any kind of fear. If I am operating in perfect love, then there is no place for fear to gain any kind of foothold or control in my life. You see, we often think that the opposite of love is hate. However, I would like to suggest that the opposite of love isn't hate; the opposite of love is fear. And fear is the breeding ground for hate. Fear is the root, and hate is the fruit.

The Scripture says it this way: "There is no fear in love. But perfect love drives out fear, because fear has to do with punishment. The one who fears is not made perfect in love" (1 John 4:18, NIV). Any time we operate in a spirit of fear, it is a sign that, in that area of our lives, love has not yet been made perfect. Another passage states it this way (as previously mentioned in Day 2): "For God has not given us a spirit of fear, but of power and of love and of a sound mind" (2 Tim. 1:7). These two Scriptures seem to indicate that fear and love are direct and polar opposites. We weren't created for fear. We were created to live in power. We were created to have a sound mind. We were created for love.

Let me show you how fear is the breeding ground for hate. I would venture to say that a vast majority of the reasons we hate something is because of our fear of that thing. For example, a student might hate school because he is afraid of failing. A wife might hate her husband because she is afraid of the next demeaning words he might say or the next unkind actions he might take. We hate getting sick because we are afraid of how sickness makes us feel.

The people who hate storms are the ones who are afraid of the destruction that might happen in the storm. The people who hate roller coasters are the ones who are afraid of how the ride will make them feel. But the people who love the storms and the rides are the ones who are not afraid of the potential outcomes.

Fear is a natural defense mechanism of our flesh that tells us to close ourselves off for our own protection. Because of this, fear prohibits us from feeling and showing love. Fear makes us resist vulnerability, and instead we cover ourselves up for our own protection. We see this pattern has existed from the beginning when Adam and Eve hid from God and covered themselves. Fear was the first result of sin entering the world. In Genesis 3:10, Adam said to God, "I heard Your voice in the garden, and I was afraid because I was naked; and I hid myself." It was out of this root of fear that men then began not only to fear God but also to hate Him. This fear and hatred toward God was an entirely different "fear" than the fear of the LORD that we are taught to show. This fear was not one of honor but one of terror. Our learned response to whatever terrorizes us is to show hatred in return.

So what, then, is our alternative? Jesus Himself told us, "Do not fear, little flock, for it is your Father's good pleasure to give you the kingdom" (Luke 12:32). When we live in fear, we forget Who our Father is. But the more we fix our gaze on our Father, the more we will live from a place of love instead of fear.

First John 4:19 tells us, "We love Him because He first loved us." Many have suggested that this verse can be interpreted as stating: "By loving us, God gave us a reason to love Him; therefore, we can choose to love Him in return." While there is some validity to this statement, I like to look at this from a slightly different angle. When we say that we love Him because He first loved us, I see it this way: "The only way we are even capable of showing any kind of love to Him is because He first showed us how to love by loving us. He loved us when we were incapable of showing Him love." Do you see the difference? We could never have loved God if He didn't love us first.

My point is this: When sin entered the world, fear entered right with it. When fear came in, it robbed us of our ability to live from a place of love. We no longer were capable of loving God or loving one another. But in spite of our insufficiencies, the Lord saw fit to show love to us, and because of His love, He has once again made us capable of showing love and living a life of love.

Is love really love if it hasn't been tested? Jesus did not only love people when He created them perfectly and they were flawless; He still loved His people in their sins, when it hurt Him the most to do so. The price of love is often manifested in pain. Jesus' love compelled Him to sacrifice His life for a people who hurt him and hated Him. It was one-sided love on His part. But because of His one-sided love, He opened the way for two-sided love to once again be restored between God and man. Jesus set the pattern for us. He loved us when we didn't love Him, so we ought to love others when they don't love us. It is for this reason that 1 John 4:16–17 says, "God is love. Whoever lives in love lives in God, and God in them. This is how love is made complete among us so that we will have confidence on the day of judgment: *In this world we are like Jesus*" (NIV, emphasis added). The best way to be like Jesus in the world is to show unconditional love, even—or especially—when it hurts.

If we live our lives doing everything we can to avoid getting hurt, then we will live a life full of fear and severely void of love. When we love, we open ourselves to hurt. But the pain is worth it. We hurt because we love, but love is still worth it. True love hurts. But it hurts a lot less than living a life of hatred rooted in fear.

The next time you choose to show love and it gets thrown back in your face, make a conscious decision to keep loving anyway. Don't set up walls so that no one can get in. Tear down the walls. Choose to love anyway. After all, you can't go wrong with love. Tell me: Can you ever be too loving? Love "always protects, always trusts, always hopes, always perseveres. Love never fails" (1 Cor. 13:7–8, NIV).

Don't be a slave to fear. Be a child of Love.

Day 4: Never Have I Seen the Righteous Forsaken

I had an interesting dream recently. In it, I remember walking outside along a semi-busy road—only, it was late at night, so the road did not have much traffic at the time. As I was walking, I saw another man walking not too far from me. We seemed to lock eyes, and then the man started coming toward me. The next thing I knew, he was trying to rob me of whatever cash I had on me. Yet, somehow, I was able to escape his grasp and get away.

Then, the dream fast forwarded to a later time. I'm not sure if it was later that same night or if it was a different night altogether. But I saw the man coming at me again. This time, I wasn't able to escape him but rather had to surrender and give him whatever money I had on me. What struck me the most was the words I spoke to the man. Very calmly but firmly and with great resolve, I said: "The joke's on you because the Lord has told me that He will repay me like one repays a loan. You will lose what you've stolen, but I will end up with more than what I had before you robbed me." The man stopped what he was doing and just looked at me. I spoke those words with great faith, and I felt absolutely no fear throughout this whole dream—only great confidence in the Lord's salvation and in His mighty power.

As I thought, prayed, and meditated about this dream, I believe the Lord's message to me was very clear: He promises to repay that which has been stolen from His children, and when He does, it will be far greater than it ever was before. And like me in the dream, we can have absolute confidence and faith in Him that He will do what He has promised and that He will always back up His word.

We are children of the most amazing Father we could ever imagine having. He does not leave His children hanging. He does not leave us lacking what we need. Every time the enemy tries to rob one of His children, He responds with vengeance and power against the enemy's attacks.

Because of who we are in Christ and because of our identity in Him, we must not succumb to the victim mentality. Being God's child doesn't mean we will never have bad things happen to us, but it does mean that whatever happens, God has our back and promises to return above and beyond that which has been stolen. Because of Christ, we are not victims. We are not slaves to fear. Even in the dark of night—even when evil seems to surround us—we shall not fear. Our Father is our defense. He is our refuge. He is our strength and fortress. And He has NEVER left the righteous forsaken (Psa. 37:25). We have such a good, good Father, and we must always take confidence in that.[vi]

Section II: Got Faith?

Day 5: Unanswered Questions

When life gives you more questions than answers, trust in God's character.

There is a reason He doesn't give us all the answers. If He did, we would stop searching. We wouldn't need to go to Him with our needs; we would already have all the answers.

Our natural bent as humans is to try to fix everything.

But when life presents us with questions we cannot find an answer to, we become so frustrated and feel like quitting.

We want to solve everything, but that's not our job.

It's God's.

Sometimes, the most helpful thing we can do is to take our problems, our unanswered questions, our brokenness, and lay them all at the feet of Jesus.

We must not quit, but we must give up—give up our right to be right, give up our pride, give up our fears, and give up our blank answers.

We aren't supposed to know all the answers. We aren't supposed to fix all the problems. What we *are* supposed to do is allow all our unanswered questions to lead us on a quest—not a quest to find the right answer, but a quest to know the Author of the question.

After all, being right with God is infinitely better than just being right.

Day 6:
Trust His Character

New Year's Day is typically one of my favorite holidays. I love the reminder that it gives us of how we can start new with a clean slate. While I'm not one to make many resolutions, I do love the idea of taking time to start the New Year right by taking intentional steps to draw nearer to the Lord. However, while I would love to say 2016 had an amazing start, I have to confess that 2016 did not begin quite like I'd hoped it would.

You see, on New Year's Day, I received three major emotional blows. That morning, my family received a phone call that our friends' son had tragically been killed as a pedestrian in a hit-and-run accident. Their son was only twenty-eight years old. My heart was deeply burdened for this family, though I didn't even know their son.

Later that day, my mom received a phone call from a specialist she had been going to for blood work, and the doctor indicated that it was a very real possibility that she could have a form of leukemia or lymphoma. My spirits sank once again. Honestly, the doctor's call left us with more questions than answers, and we were at a loss for how to respond or what to do next.

My family chose to respond in worship unto the Lord, and during this worship time, we sounded the alarm and sent out many notes for prayer. I sent out some prayer request emails and texts, and one of my friends wrote back that he would be praying, but he also asked for prayer because he was going in for a scan because the doctors were concerned he had a tumor on his brain. My heart sank even lower.

Happy New Year! Your friends' son died, your mom might have a serious disease, and your friend might have a brain tumor. This was not the way I wanted to start 2016.

Prior to this time, I had been meditating a lot on how good God is and how grateful I was for His many blessings. "Good Good Father" had become a favorite song of mine to sing, coupled with "No Longer Slaves." With that, I was also dwelling a lot on living free from fear and instead full of power like the Lord intended. However, when everything seemed to start caving in, it became more difficult to sing about the Lord being a "Good Good Father." It became more difficult to sing, "I'm no longer a slave to fear." My fears were colliding with my faith.

Through it all, however, one particular phrase stood out to me that another friend had texted me: he told me to trust God's character. Even when things don't make sense, and even when we want to give up and walk away, we have to trust that God's character never changes. You see, it's easy to call him a "Good Good Father" when everything is going well, but what about when everything seems to fall to pieces? Is He still good? Can we still trust His character?

I have to be real and confess that it took me a while before I could again utter those words: "You are good, Lord. You are good." Yet, I finally came to the conclusion that I had to trust His character, no matter what. My faith compelled me to overcome my fear. Nothing on the outside changed, but the Lord changed my outlook. He helped me to see things from a new perspective. Life is not always good, but God always is, and He is always faithful. I can trust in His character, no matter what.

  And you know what? Even in the tragedy of my friends' son dying, through his death, I was able to learn of the amazing life He lived and the thousands of people he impacted for Christ in his twenty-eight-year lifespan. This didn't take away the pain of his loss, but it certainly added volumes to the testimony of his life. Amazing. Also, I learned a few days later that my friend had no tumors in his brain. It was all just a scare over nothing. I praised God for that. Finally, I began to see my mom climb to new heights in her faith, and her faith inspired me to push forward in faith as well, trusting that the Lord indeed has her healing already taken care of, because, after all, He is good…always.

  The year may not have started the way I wanted, but in the end, I know the results will be victorious and that they will draw me closer to the goodness of God than I ever have been before. I choose to trust in the character of my God, no matter what. He is faithful and true. He will never let me down.

Day 7:
Where's Your Faith?

Faith often gets a bad rep these days simply because of certain preconceived notions and stereotypes. For instance, when many people hear the word *faith*, they begin to think of a time when someone told them, "If you just had more faith, then you wouldn't have this problem," or, "You didn't get healed because you just didn't have enough faith." Of course, while the people who say this might mean well, their concept of faith is so far from the truth.

Having said that, the right response is not to ignore the concept of faith or to run the other direction. Rather, the right response is to gain a proper understanding of what faith really is.

Put simply, our faith has the power to move the heart of God. Let that sink in for a moment. We know that without faith it is impossible to please God (Heb. 11:6), so it follows naturally that when we do respond in faith, we are operating in a capacity and realm that is very pleasing to God.

I want to be numbered among the people who actually moved God's heart because of their faith. I want to be included with people like Abraham, Moses, and Mary. When God was ready to completely wipe out a wicked city, Abraham had the faith to stand in the gap between God and the people and intercede.[vii] He moved the heart of God in such a way that God agreed to spare the city if even as few as ten righteous people could be found in it—but alas, not even ten were found.

Likewise, Moses moved the heart of God by having the faith to intercede on behalf of the rebellious Israelite people.[viii] When the Israelites turned away from the Lord, God wanted to destroy them all. But because of Moses' faith and intercession, he actually moved the heart of God in such a way that God decided to spare the people.

Of course, we all love the story of Mary. When a miracle was needed during the wedding at Cana, Jesus told Mary that it was not yet His time to work miracles.[ix] However, Mary's response of faith moved God's heart in a profound way when she instructed the servants to obey whatever Jesus said. Within moments, what was formerly the wrong time became exactly the right time.

Mary's faith moved the heart of God. Moses' faith moved the heart of God. Abraham's faith moved the heart of God. And our faith will move the heart of God too. So my question for you is: Where is your faith? What are you believing God for? Are your expectations and desires too low? Are you pressing in for God's highest and His best?

Jesus' disciples made a simple request of Jesus: that Jesus would increase their faith.[x] And He did. Let that now be our request too. After all, the same faith that has the power to move mountains also has the power to move the heart of God. And the same power that raised Jesus from the dead now works in you.[xi]

Day 8:
Have Faith, My Friends

We say that faith without works is dead. We say that faith the size of a mustard seed can move a mountain. Actually, God said both of those things before we ever did (Jas. 2:26; Matt. 17:19–20). But what do those things really mean? Does faith require such grand and amazing mountain-moving works on our part? What does faith look like, anyway?

Dead faith sees a mountain and does nothing about it. Dead faith runs away in the other direction. Dead faith has no initiative. Dead faith expects a handout. There is not even a mustard seed of action when only dead faith is involved. Mustard seed faith, on the other hand, is an entirely different story. Faith without works is dead, but a mustard seed of faith is very alive. A tiny living seed can accomplish far more than a giant dead tree!

Oftentimes, we discredit our own faith because it doesn't look like much, if anything. However, God does not tell us that mustard seed faith is dead. Mustard seed faith is alive. The only type of faith that is dead is faith that is completely devoid of any type of corresponding works whatsoever. The tiniest mustard seed of faith is enough to move a mountain because the tiniest mustard seed of faith is very much alive.

What does mustard seed faith look like? Many times, it looks like a simple glance toward God, a one-word prayer, or a simple heart cry. The times when we have a mustard seed of faith are the times when we feel we are at our lowest—like we have nothing in us to give. It seems like we have no words to pray, like we have nothing valuable to contribute. Yet, at those moments, mustard seed faith reveals itself in our lives when we simply take a step and *do*...something. Anything. A word. A song. A simple gesture. Something to indicate that we haven't completely given up hope.

Sometimes, the mountain we are facing seems so huge that the only thing we can say is, "God, help." We can't even get anything else out at that moment. But the amazing thing is that God recognizes the mustard seed of faith inside us, and that is all it takes to get a mountain to move out of the way.

The next time you face a mountain, don't discredit the mustard seed of faith that you have. You might not take a leap of faith. It might not even be a step. It might be a tiny tiptoe forward, but it is still progress, and it still demonstrates faith and trust in the Lord just by that tiny movement. Take that tiny step, and watch how God will use that step to strengthen you to take another, and another, and another. Pretty soon, you will find that either the mountain has moved or God has strengthened you to climb right over it! Either way, it all begins with a decision: A decision not to do nothing. A decision to take a step, no matter how small it may be, and see what God will do. A decision like that will not go unnoticed, and it will not go unrewarded.

Watch out: I have a mustard seed of faith, and I'm not afraid to use it!

Have faith, my friends. Have faith.

Day 9:
FAITH | RISK

When I reflect on my life and what the Lord has been showing me, I am compelled to take note of the amazing things that happen when I choose to take a risk—to take a step of faith and trust God with the results. My natural tendency in life is to want to play it safe. If I find a method that works, why should I change it? After all, if it ain't broke, don't fix it—right?

Actually, wrong.

If it ain't broke, it might be because it ain't broke *yet*; however, we need to be in tune with the way things are going and what will happen if we continue indefinitely on the same route we're on. Just because something works now, it doesn't mean it will work forever. For this reason, we need to be intentional about stepping out of the box and doing things in unconventional ways. Unconventional responses lead to uncomfortable results; yet, these feelings of discomfort are good and healthy and drive us to greater success.

Why wait until something breaks before you fix it? Why not proactively find a better way to do something ahead of time so that the thing will not break in the first place? A prime example of this is when my church decided to change the structure of its services. We had previously been having one full worship set of four to five songs prior to the sermon, but my father, who is the pastor, felt led to change the order to having two songs, then a break for testimonies, and then two more songs. I didn't like this change at first because I felt like what we were doing was working well. However, just because something is a *good* option, it doesn't mean it is the *best* option. When we made the change, I discovered that having the break was beneficial to help the worship team regroup, give people a chance to sit down for a few minutes, and to add the valuable aspect of sharing testimonies to our service, which we previously did not have. Rather than waiting for something to come up, we proactively looked for a better way, even though it meant doing things differently and getting a bit uncomfortable. In hindsight, I am very glad we made this change.

The Lord has challenged me many times to stretch myself and do uncomfortable things. He has been revealing to me the value of taking risks. And you know what? Some of my greatest victories in life have come out of some of my greatest risks. You know what else? Some of my greatest failures have also come out of my greatest risks. However, the key to rebounding from these failures is to give ourselves more grace, not take ourselves too seriously, and say at the end of the day, "Well, at least I tried! And I'll do better next time!" At my home church, Kingdom Encounters, we say it this way: It is better to try, fail, and try again than never to have tried at all.

Our perfection-minded society has put a damper on our ability to take risks. We fear risks because we fear failure. However, one of the best ways to learn is to fail—and then try again. Rather than pointing fingers at each other when we fail after taking a risk, we should have an entirely different attitude. We should honor one another and commend each other for trying. We need to do a much better job of creating safe environments for one another to take risks—to take steps of faith. How many times do we point our fingers at Peter because he started sinking while he walked on the water? Have we forgotten that he was the only one bold enough to take the risk and get out of the boat?

Having experienced the joys and trials of taking risks, my goal is to continue moving forward with an attitude of taking more risks and conquering my fears. John Maxwell wrote a book called *Failing Forward*, and his title so accurately depicts the goal: that even failure can propel me forward in the direction of greater learning and growth. In that, my goal is also to create an atmosphere wherever I go where it is safe for others to do the same. With this perspective, it is more important for me to celebrate the process than the outcome.

We too often confuse excellence and perfectionism. Excellence is doing everything to the best of our ability, to the glory of God. Perfectionism is doing everything we can to protect our image. We can't take risks with an attitude of perfectionism, but we certainly can and should take risks with an attitude of excellence. When we have an attitude of excellence, we will take risks with excellence. At times, we will fail with excellence. But ultimately, we will learn, grow, and succeed with excellence.

What do I mean by failing with excellence? I mean that, rather than seeing failure as an end, we see it as a stepping stone to a new beginning. Failing with excellence means that we don't let anything keep us down. Instead, we learn, we grow, and we continue to step out, take risks, and allow the Lord to develop His character in us. Approaching failure in this way leads to success, because it carries with it an attitude of "Don't quit!" The real failure doesn't come from stepping out and messing up. The real failure comes from refusing to step out in the first place. So what is the conclusion? Ask yourself today: What risks might God want me to take? In what ways is He calling me to step out, and what is hindering me from doing so? As you discover the answer to those questions, there is only one thing left to do: Take the leap of faith, and trust God with the outcome. Trust me—you won't regret it!

Day 10: Miracles

We love to sing the lyrics of a popular worship song that says, "A miracle can happen now, for the Spirit of the Lord is here. The evidence is all around that the Spirit of the Lord is here."[xii] But do we really believe it? Do we really believe miracles still happen? Sure, they might happen for some famous preacher or at some popular worship concert. They might happen overseas with global workers and missionaries in third world countries. We certainly have no problem believing that the miracles in the Bible really happened. But can a miracle happen in our lives—right here and right now? Somehow, we have more trouble believing this.

But if we're willing to sing about it, then we need to believe it.

We love studying Jesus' miracles in the Bible. He turned water into wine. He healed the lame man who was lowered through the roof. He demonstrated power over nature by calming a violent storm with a single word. He fed five thousand men (plus women and children) with only five loaves of bread and two fish. He even walked on water to show how powerful He is!

If Jesus demonstrated His power through His miracles in the Bible times, who are we to believe that He ever stopped? The book of Hebrews teaches us that "Jesus Christ is the same yesterday, today, and forever" (13:8). The same Jesus who did miracles in the Bible is the same Jesus Who can and will do them today!

What are you praying for? What are you believing God for? Did you know that your faith can actually move the heart of God to do the miraculous? No, this does not mean that we can have any kind of control over God. Nor does it mean that if miracles don't happen, it's because we didn't have enough faith. Neither of the above are aligned with a biblical perspective. However, what this does mean is that there definitely is something to be said about the power of our faith.[xiii]

Think about Jesus' first miracle, which I have already referenced in the devotion for Day 7.[xiv] When Jesus' mother Mary came to Him and informed Him that the wine had run out, His response was basically: "That's not My problem!" He knew it was not yet time for His miraculous ministry to begin. Yet, within seconds, His time had suddenly come! Why? Because Mary demonstrated her great faith, telling the servants to do whatever Jesus told them to do. Mary knew Who Jesus was, and she knew what Jesus could do; and the demonstration of her faith moved the heart of God in such a way that it propelled Him into beginning His earthly ministry. That's powerful.

Other people have moved God's heart throughout history as well. For example, God was planning to annihilate and completely do away with the people of Israel, but Moses' prayers and faith led God to change His mind and spare the people from death.[xv] Likewise, King Hezekiah prayed and contended with God, convincing Him to add more years to his life.[xvi]

What's the point?

The point is that we too often set our expectations way too low. Call me crazy, but sometimes, I think God *wants* us to change His mind. But in order to do that, we have to step out in faith. We need to be like Mary, who would not take "no" for an answer. She asked Jesus for a miracle, Jesus said, "No," and then she proceeded to prepare for the miracle as if He had said yes. And guess what? His *no* changed to *yes* because of the activation of her faith.

Certainly, there are many times when God's "no" is a firm "NO." But have you ever wondered if sometimes we give up too easily? The first time a prayer isn't answered, we stop praying. When someone we know needs a miracle, and the situation actually gets worse instead of better, we tend to lose faith and give up hope. But what if we're missing an opportunity when this happens—an opportunity to press in a little harder, to pray until something happens, and to persevere until we see a breakthrough? We cannot give up at the first sign of defeat. The men with their paralyzed friend did not give up when they could not get into the house where Jesus was teaching. They just found another way and lowered him through the roof.

When we are praying to God for a miracle, do we actually believe He can do the miraculous? Do we actually believe He *will* do the miraculous? We know that God is sovereign—that He is God over everything and has complete control and authority. We know that He sometimes answers "yes" and sometimes "no." But if you take anything away from this devotional, take this: Don't be too quick to take "no" for an answer. Don't back down at the first sign of defeat or struggle. That is when you need to press in all the more. Pray like you never prayed before. Believe that God is working through those prayers. Expect a miracle. And realize that the miracle might not look like what you thought it would look like—but it will be good.

When I was in high school, I developed significant lower back pain for reasons unknown to me. I prayed numerous times for healing and also had a number of other people pray over me, yet nothing changed. However, one night in youth group, I received prayer from my youth pastors, and I was overcome by the power of God and fell to the floor. When I got up, the back pain was gone! Now, in the natural, falling usually leads to a *greater* injury, not a healing! But God used the falling experience to actually bring healing to my body. Explain that one! The miracle came, not right away, but over time and in a way I didn't expect it. This is a prime example of why we must continue to press in for a breakthrough and be open to whatever unusual way that breakthrough might come.

Finally, when it all is said and done, regardless of the outcome—praise God in all circumstances. Trust His character. Know that He works all things together according to His divine purposes. Live like you believe it.

Section III: The Battle on Our Knees

Day 11
Prayer—The Long and Short of It

In the Christian faith, we come upon a variety of dichotomies with which we wrestle. I have been musing about one particular contrast recently. It is the distinction between pressing into God in faith and waiting patiently upon God in faith. On one hand, we are taught to pray without ceasing, to press in for a miracle, and to "ask and keep on asking,"[xvii] demonstrating our faith that we will not give up until the breakthrough comes. It's exemplified in the story of Jacob when he wrestled with God and would not let God go until He pronounced His blessing upon Jacob (Gen. 32:22–32). We also know the parable about the importunate woman who would not stop confronting the judge until he gave in and gave her what she was asking for (Luke 18:1–8). Certainly, there is Scriptural backing for relentless, passionate prayer.

Yet, there is also Scriptural evidence for something that seems quite the opposite. We are told by Jesus not to pray prayers that are any longer than necessary (Matt. 6:5–15). When we pray lengthy prayers with lengthy words, we point attention to ourselves and away from God, and we also seem to take matters into our own hands rather than trusting

God with the answer. We know God hears us the first time we pray; therefore, what is the purpose or need to continue laboring in prayer if He heard the first time?

I believe these two teachings both have strong biblical and Scriptural support; yet, if that is so, why do they seem to contradict each other? I would submit that these do not conflict with each other as they seem to—rather, they are two sides of the same coin. Praying repeatedly and importunately demonstrates great faith on our part, because it says we won't take "no" for an answer. Likewise, praying one short, simple prayer with full trust in God demonstrates great faith on our part because we know that God hears us the first time and that He promises to answer.

The key question to ask regarding prayer, therefore, becomes not "how" should I pray, but "why" am I praying this way? Am I praying a long prayer repeatedly because I'm not giving up until I see breakthrough? Or am I praying this long prayer to be impressive or because I don't have the faith to believe God heard me the first time?

Similarly, when praying short prayers, we must ask pertinent questions. Am I praying this prayer once in a short and succinct format because I believe God hears me and I have peace in my spirit to know that the answer is coming? Or did I stop short because I lost my enthusiasm or energy to give the effort this matter deserved?

These are difficult questions to discern the answers. However, the answers to these questions will help determine whether we are on the right track in the particular mode of prayer that we are practicing at that moment.

A final and important thought to add is that we must be led by the Lord to know how He is asking us to pray in that particular moment. John 5:19 says that Jesus only did what He saw the Father doing. There were times when He spoke prayers that were very short (John 11:41–42), but there were other times when He labored all night in prayer (Luke 6:12).

Bottom line: When it comes to prayer, don't make assumptions. Don't assume that you need to pray all night if a simple prayer of faith would do. But don't conclude you can get by with a short prayer when the issue merits much greater perseverance in prayer. Ask the Lord to lead you as you pray, and trust that He will show you!

Day 12:
Less Talk—More Prayer

I'm going to make a revolutionary proposal: What if we spent less time talking about our problems and more time praying about them? And by praying about them, I don't mean "gossip-praying" about them; I mean sincerely giving these things to God and laying them at His feet in prayer. I am convinced that if we took the time we spent complaining, lamenting, and gossiping about our problems and instead filled that time with prayer, we would not be in nearly the amount of messes we find ourselves in.

Pastor Latosha Johnson, [xviii] who was my youth pastor when I was in high school, recently made the following statement:

> Our prayers do not fall on deaf ears. It's our responsibility to pray more than just talking about all that is going on. If we just talk about it, it can become draining…but if we pray about it, it produces life and transformation…. "The Lord is near to all who call on Him, to all who call on Him in truth." –Psalm 145:8.

Wow, how true and powerful those words are. The problems in our nation will not go away by us talking and grumbling about them. They just won't. In fact, when we do that, the only thing we do is add fuel to a fire. Yes, there are times to voice our opinions and concerns and defend our rights—but that's not what I'm talking about here. I'm talking about excessive, useless complaining, grumbling, and whining. It just doesn't produce anything healthy—at all.

The same is true for our relationships, our jobs, our schools, our churches…the list goes on and on. What if we stopped our useless chatter and instead began genuinely, reverently, and passionately praying for the Lord's intervention and deliverance in these dire situations?

It is a sad thing to say, but many Christians are better at talking than they are at praying. But their talking yields no healthy fruit. Instead of talking about the problem, how about we do something about it? How about we start praying? I'm talking about more than just absent-minded token prayers. I'm talking about real, genuine, tangible prayers—prayers that produce fruit, prayers that leave a legacy.

Who's with me? Let's do it.

Day 13:
Biblical Problem Solving

One big problem facing the church today is that some people have grown to rely more upon programs of man rather than the power of the Holy Spirit. Some have become far more reliant on man-made solutions and have begun to forget the importance of prayer. This is actually very serious and very dangerous because it causes us to rely on our own strength (which always fails us) instead of the power of the Holy Spirit (which never fails).

No plan of any church can be consistently successful without the strong backing of prayer. Sure, a program or strategy might lead to success for a time without prayer, but it will not produce lasting fruit without the strong backing of prayer and intercession. It is such a dangerous thing when we begin to rely more on the programs of man rather than prayer and the power of the Holy Spirit.

Without prayer and the anointing, the programs of man are just grasping at straws. Without the power of the Holy Spirit, all of our programs, plans, and agendas are just wastes of time. We in this society have become really good at talking and using the right words at the right time. Yet, God said that His kingdom is not a kingdom of words alone, but also a kingdom of power (1 Cor. 4:20).

I do not mean that talking is all bad. But I do mean that we spend so much more time analyzing, discussing, talking, and evaluating problems and how to solve them than we do praying, pressing in, interceding, and listening to the voice of the Holy Spirit for His solutions. To what avail? We talk about how to solve the problems of the world, but do we invite the Holy Spirit into our conversations?

It is frustrating to see the church go around the same circles over and over again, slapping a new face and a new name onto an old strategy or program. Some have said that the definition of insanity is doing the same thing over and over but expecting different results. How much of this have we allowed to creep in?

Maybe if we spent as much time praying as we did programming, we would actually see change. Perhaps if we gathered together in unity and put aside our differences to come together in a united front of consistent prayer, worship, intercession, and devotion, we would actually see transformation. Certainly, if we repented of our pride, rebellion, and idolatry, we would actually see revival in our midst.

Talking about problems doesn't change things. Developing man-made programs to fix the problems doesn't change things. Coming together in unity through prayer, repentance, and worship—now that, my friends, is what changes things.

Let's join together in unity and humility, trusting that God will bring the increase.

Day 14:
The Battle

I wonder what life would be like if we could see in the spirit realm—to see the spiritual battles going on all around us. Don't get me wrong: I'm not saying I want to be able to see that all the time; however, to get a simple glimpse of the realities of spiritual warfare would be a really eye-opening experience.

What is going on in the spiritual realm around a person—or even inside a person—when they're being faced with temptation, with doubt, with fear, or with deep sorrow or depression? What type of spiritual battle is going on when a person is sitting in front of a computer, on the verge of making one click that could change his or her life for the worse? What form of spiritual conflict would we see when two people who used to be good friends start arguing and fighting over their own selfish motives? Would we see angels and demons fighting with flaming swords? Would we see a big blob of darkness coming up against a giant orb of light?

The Bible says that "our struggle is not against flesh and blood, but against the rulers, against the authorities, against the powers of this dark world and against the spiritual forces of evil in the heavenly realms" (Eph. 6:12, NIV). We are in a very real battle. In fact, the battle in the spiritual realm is more real than any battle we could ever face in the natural realm. Yet because we cannot see this spiritual battle, we tend to end up fighting the wrong thing—or even worse, we forget we are even in a battle at all. We are to fight against "spiritual forces of evil in the heavenly realms," but we too often direct our aim against things in the natural world—namely, people. But people are not our enemies. Whenever we use our efforts to fight against other people instead of fighting against our true enemies, the devil and the powers of darkness, we are ultimately focusing our efforts on entirely the wrong thing.

The enemy loves nothing more than when he can successfully lead us into temptation and cause us to stumble. The Scripture is clear about this in several places. Did you know that immediately before Cain killed his brother Abel, God spoke to him and said, "If you do not do what is right, sin is crouching at your door; it desires to have you, but you must rule over it" (Gen. 4:7b, NIV)? Likewise, Jesus said this to Simon Peter just before Simon Peter denied Him three times: "Simon, Simon, satan has asked to sift all of you as wheat. But I have prayed for you, Simon, that your faith may not fail" (Luke 22:31–32a, NIV).

In other words, what God was saying to Cain and to Simon Peter was that the opportunity to sin is always right in front of us. As long as we are on this earth, we are always only one decision away from sinning. And when we don't take the battle that we are in seriously, it becomes that much easier to fall into sin.

Jesus said to His followers, "Pray that you will not fall into temptation" (Luke 22:40b, NIV). From this we know that we are supposed to fervently and regularly pray that God would keep us from the attacks and snares of the enemy. But beyond that, we know that we are not alone in this prayer of intercession, for, "Christ Jesus…is at the right hand of God and is also interceding for us" (Rom. 8:34, NIV). This is so encouraging, because it is from this passage that we know we are not in this battle alone. Jesus is fighting on our behalf as well!

So how are we to respond? We must trust that Jesus is fighting on our behalf, but we must also take seriously the battle that we are in. Even though we cannot see the battle, it is more real than anything we can see on this earth. Therefore, we must dress daily for battle, putting on the full armor of God, which includes: truth, righteousness, peace, faith, salvation, God's Word, and prayer. These are the weapons of our warfare. We must learn to use them—not to attack other people, but to defeat the wicked schemes of the devil and the forces of darkness.

Day 15:
Find Your Aaron and Hur

A few years ago, I sensed the Lord gave me a very specific word for my life. What I sensed was that He was telling me that I needed to have a small group of people in my life who would be to me like Aaron and Hur were to Moses. If you don't know what this means, it refers to an account from the Old Testament book of Exodus. The Israelites were fighting against the Amalekites, according to the Lord's instructions. The Lord gave them a very sure way to know if they would have victory or not. Read Exodus 17:11–13 for the full details:

> And so it was, when Moses held up his hand, that Israel prevailed; and when he let down his hand, Amalek prevailed. But Moses' hands became heavy; so they took a stone and put it under him, and he sat on it. And Aaron and Hur supported his hands, one on one side, and the other on the other side; and his hands were steady until the going down of the sun. So Joshua defeated Amalek and his people with the edge of the sword.

What I sensed God was saying to me through this was that I was going to face battles in my life, and I would need to be able to keep my hands directed toward heaven throughout these battles. However, if I tried to do this with my own strength, I would fail. I must have people in my life who would act like Aaron and Hur, holding up my hands when I don't have the strength to do it on my own. This has come to be such a vital part of my walk with the Lord.

Another Scripture puts it this way: "Though one may be overpowered by another, two can withstand him. And a threefold cord is not quickly broken" (Ecc. 4:12). One of the lies the enemy often speaks to God's children is that they just need to buckle down and do it. So many people try to bear their burdens alone, thinking they have enough strength within them to see them through; but they don't. God's plan is by design: We must have people in our lives who can build us up when we're down and support us when we're fighting. Thus, we must open ourselves up to trust these people as we invite them into our lives.

For me, this has made all the difference. Just around the time I was writing this, I was feeling strong oppression from the enemy. Unfortunately, I did not reach out for help the first couple days; I wish I would have. However, by the third day, it finally dawned on me that I needed to reach out for prayer. I asked several prayer warriors for support, and very soon after that, I began to feel the oppression lift. It felt like a new day.

Through all of this, I have learned that, when I am struggling, I need to reach out to someone I trust who will pray for me and encourage me. I have learned that I do not have enough strength within myself to keep my own hands up for the entire duration of the battle. I am so thankful the Lord has blessed me with several Aarons and Hurs in my life, and I am also thankful to be an Aaron/Hur to others.

Don't try to go it alone. Your mission is too important and your life is too valuable for you to try to fight your battles with your own strength. Trust the Lord for His strength, yes, but also trust the Lord to send you godly individuals who can strengthen you and build you up as they keep your arms directed toward Heaven. This will make a heavenly world of difference.

Section IV: Learning (The Easy Way)

Day 16:
The Learning Curve

Every day, when I teach my students at school, I am inspired and deeply blessed by their passion and excitement about learning. They so frequently pull on me and what I have to impart to them, asking deep questions, searching for greater understanding, and showing high engagement in discussions. They seem to have this innate desire to always learn more, and they demonstrate a true love for learning.

So where along the road do we lose this? The more I am around my students, the more I am convicted that, somewhere along the line, I began to look at learning differently than I did when I was younger. When I was young, learning was an exciting process filled with endless possibilities. As I grew older, it seemed to become more of a mundane routine that required work and constructive correction.

People have a tendency to lose their love for learning as they grow older. Children are so excited to try new things, and they aren't as concerned about the amount of work involved or the amount of correction they will need to receive in the process. Adults, on the other hand, seem to shy away from learning because either (a) they don't want to invest the effort anymore or (b) they fear the necessary correction that comes through the process. To be truly teachable, you have to surrender your own agenda and timetable and instead allow yourself to be guided through the learning process.

Effective learning requires a measure of humility on the part of the learner. Certainly, children deal with their own issues of pride too; however, there seems to be an aspect of innocence and humility in many children that slowly fades away as they get older. It's like, once people graduate from high school or college, they think they somehow automatically now know it all and don't need to learn anymore. They are too old for that.

I am learning to take a lesson from the children I teach: No matter how old we are, we must never lose our love for learning. Since when did learning become a chore, anyway? Why do we love the word *learning* when we are children, but we come to reject it as adults? Just like it was designed to be in elementary school, learning is supposed to be fun! If it isn't, then we're doing it wrong.

Let's challenge ourselves to once again surrender to the joy, excitement, and adventures of learning!

Day 17:
Figuring It Out

Why do we always try to figure everything out? Because we want control over our situations? Because we worry and fret if we don't understand what's happening? Because in order for something to be right, it must be logical? One thing I know is this: It's not inherently wrong for us to try to figure things out. Proverbs 25:2 says, "It is the glory of God to conceal a thing: but the honour of kings is to search out a matter" (KJV). It is a natural human tendency to search out the hidden matters of God. We like to figure things out. And God likes for us to figure things out... to a point.

However, the boundary line has been crossed when we begin to be consumed with relying upon our own understanding. Proverbs also tells us, "Trust in the Lord with all your heart, and lean not on your own understanding" (3:5). It's one thing to try to search out the deep mysteries of God out of motivation to know Him more and gain a greater, more accurate understanding of Who He is. Yet, it's another thing to try to figure out what He is doing when it is not our business to know. God is God, and we, in our flesh, are not. God's ways are higher than our ways (Isa. 55:9).

So many of us try to make everything about life make perfect sense. Yet, if we are constantly trying to do that, we should ask ourselves why we are even Christians. Think about it. Being a Christian makes absolutely no sense in the eyes of the world. We worship a God we cannot see. We believe in a God who died, but also rose again. We believe that this act saved us from the eternal punishment of sin if we will believe in Him. This also requires us to believe that we actually are sinful and need someone to save us. Does this all sound ludicrous? In man's eyes, it is. Yet, every Christian believes this. Why, then, do Christians not believe other aspects of God's Word which, in my opinion, are far easier to believe than what I just described above?

For instance, we often have such a hard time believing God actually can and will provide for our needs. Yet, if He cares about our eternity, do you not think He also cares about our daily lives? We have a hard time believing He can heal us of our diseases. Yet, which is more difficult: to heal someone physically or to heal someone spiritually? For those who are in Christ, He has already brought healing to our spiritual lives. The proof is that once we were dead, but now we are alive in Him (Eph. 2:1–5). Not only is this an act of divine spiritual healing, but it is a full-blown act of resurrection power!

My point is this: Why can we believe in the doctrine of salvation (which is foolishness to the world [1 Cor. 1:18]) but not believe that God cares and works sovereignly in the more minute aspects of our lives? The reason we do not always believe this is because it doesn't make sense in our natural eyes. We still see life through the eyes of "every man for himself." Somehow, we have to think through everything and make sure it makes sense to us before we act on it. Yet, if the foundation of our belief system is foolishness in the eyes of the world, what makes us think that the rest of our lives have to make sense to the world? If our foundation is foolishness to the world, then our whole lives should, in a sense, be foolishness to the world.

I'm not saying we shouldn't use wisdom, logic, or sound judgment. God clearly calls us to use wisdom all throughout Scripture. The book of Proverbs is a primary example. Yet, we must not confuse godly wisdom with the wisdom of the world. The wisdom of the world "does not descend from above, but is earthly, sensual, demonic. For where envy and self-seeking exist, confusion and every evil thing are there. But the wisdom that is from above is first pure, then peaceable, gentle, willing to yield, full of mercy and good fruits, without partiality and without hypocrisy" (Jas. 3:15–17).

My challenge to you today is this: Learn to distinguish the difference between the wisdom of the world and the wisdom of God. Live according to God's wisdom, not the world's wisdom. God's wisdom causes you to seek Him out in order to gain a deeper understanding of Who He is and how to live for Him. Man's wisdom causes you to lean on your own understanding and figure everything out apart from Him. Don't live that way. Choose God's wisdom today and every day.

Day 18: Evidence

> *"Now faith is the substance of things hoped for, the evidence of things not seen....But without faith it is impossible to please Him, for he who comes to God must believe that He is, and that He is a rewarder of those who diligently seek Him."*
>
> ~Hebrews 11:1, 6

We talk a lot about evidence for why the Bible is true. There are so many undeniable truths, facts, records, and documents that all point toward the truth and reality of Scripture. Yet, in the midst of all the evidence, we cannot deny the fact that there are still some things in the Scripture that we cannot explain. I mean, was a man really swallowed by a giant fish and then vomited onto land on the third day? Come on! Does God really expect us to believe that? Well, yes, He does.

But here's the thing: While the evidence of Scripture is overwhelmingly true, there is still a place where we must accept certain things by faith. In fact, the Scripture above tells us that faith itself *is* evidence! Now, how can that be true? How can my faith in God actually *be* evidence that proves He exists? I'll tell you how.

Faith is "the evidence of things not seen" because faith is like an internal compass in our hearts that always points us back to God. If we don't have faith, then we will purely rely on our minds to point us toward all the natural evidences for God. Yet, if we only rely on our minds, we will end up turning away from God at the first moment that something in our walk with God does not make sense. However, if we have faith, we will be able to follow and trust God, even when things do not make sense. Our faith in God continues to point our hearts toward Him even in the most difficult moments, like when we see extreme suffering in the world, when we deal with a tragic loss of a loved one, or when we encounter another type of crisis in life. People who believe in God only with their *minds* will turn away from Him in these circumstances, but people who believe in their *hearts* will stay true to Him, no matter what.

Faith is evidence in itself because faith relies on the power of our testimony. Revelation 12:11 tells us that believers overcome "by the blood of the Lamb and by the word of their testimony." In other words, we overcome the devices of satan and the lies of the world when we choose to stand firm on the unique testimony that each of us has regarding our walks with God. Every time we tell our testimony to others or even simply remind ourselves, we are building faith in our hearts and the hearts of those who hear. Each believer's testimony is powerful, and no one can argue with it! This is why it is so important, when sharing about Jesus with people, not only to quote Scripture, but also to tell them how Jesus has impacted our lives personally. That, my friends, is evidence beyond doubt. When nothing else makes sense in life, our testimonies will still stand.

So put your faith in God. Study to show yourself approved. Learn all the evidences for the Scripture. Learn the reasons to believe the Bible and the resurrection. Learn how to debunk the myths and false teachings people have tried to proclaim against the Bible. But above all else, know the evidence in your own heart—the evidence that comes from a life of faith in Jesus and a testimony that no one can ever take away from you! People can tamper with and destroy physical evidence, but no one can ever steal your faith and your testimony of your relationship with Jesus.

Section V:
This One's for All the Control Freaks...

Day 19:
Eternity Calling

"He has made everything beautiful in its time. He has also set eternity in the human heart; yet no one can fathom what God has done from beginning to end."

~Ecclesiastes 3:11

Have you ever really stopped to just think about eternity? I mean really think about it? When we truly contemplate the reality that we will live eternally, it is a concept that has the potential to blow our minds. But the reality is true: We were made for eternity! God never created us with the intention that we would someday perish. Sin is what brought death into the world, but that was never God's intent. The Scripture above states that "He has also set eternity in the human heart." This means that, in our hearts, we have a longing to live eternally. There is something in us that points us toward a greater reality than we currently comprehend.

Because of this truth, I would venture to say that everyone on the earth has a longing somewhere deep down in their hearts to experience the reality of eternity. I think that even those who would not admit to this desire, such as atheists, still do have some sort of longing for eternity deep down in their hearts. This is because we are created with this longing, whether we realize or agree with it or not!

And think about this: The reality of eternity is much greater than our present reality. Many of the things we think are so important right now won't even matter at all when we stand face-to-face with eternity. The Scripture, in James 4:14, tells us: "Why, you do not even know what will happen tomorrow. What is your life? You are a mist that appears for a little while and then vanishes." Yet, how we live this "mist" of a life profoundly affects how we will spend our eternal destiny.

So, what is your choice? When you reach the end of your life and look back, what did you do with the "mist" you were given? How much of it did you waste away? How much of it was spent on your phone, your iPad, your video games, or your television? How much of it was spent in quality time with your family? How much of it was spent in quality time with God and in leading others to Him? We will have to give an account of our lives before God.

The Scripture states that the parts of our life that were wasted away will be burned up like fire at the end (1 Cor. 3:13–15). When we get to the end, what will we have to show for it? What will the Lord say to us? I want to make my life on this earth count for as much as possible. This life on the earth is so short as it is; I don't have time to waste. It's time for the people of God to live with an eternal perspective, making every moment count, and glorifying God through everything. After all, this is what truly matters.

Day 20: Transform Us

Did you know that it's possible to change but still remain the same? That doesn't seem to make sense, but many people do this very thing. They may change a lot of things, but deep down, they are the same people they always were. Many of us say we want revival or transformation, but we are unwilling to allow God to transform us personally. We act like we're changed, we talk like we're changed, but we're still the same on the inside as we've always been.

Take a house, for example. You can paint that house, give it a facelift, and redo the landscaping. But it's still a house. What would have to happen to change the identity of that house? Either (a) its structure would have to drastically change, or (b) its function would have to change. There are people who operate businesses out of what used to be houses. In each instance, the building is no longer a house, but a barbershop, an attorney's office, a restaurant, etc. Make sense so far?

The identity of a thing has not been changed until its usage has been changed. So, what's our identity? It's all too easy for people to put on a front, but their identity has not changed. Are we living our lives for the things of God or the things of the world? The Bible says that when one truly accepts Christ, he is a new creation (2 Cor. 5:17). True transformation has not occurred in an individual's life unless he or she has literally become a new person in Christ. Romans 12:2 reads this way out of the NIV:

> Do not conform any longer to the pattern of this world, but be transformed by the renewing of your mind. Then you will be able to test what God's will is—His good, pleasing, and perfect will.

Notice that this Scripture does not simply say, "Be changed." Change implies an outward adjustment without an identity shift. Transformation gets at the very core of an identity! Interestingly, when we talk about change, we find that we have to be more specific. In the Bible, two words describe change. The *first* one implies a total and drastic life change, as in the metamorphosis of a caterpillar to a butterfly. It literally means to "change forms" (aka transform)! But the *second* one refers to the partial change of a thing, typically affecting the external or outside realm only. In other words, this is a *disguise*. Do you see how both words referring to change have two completely different and nearly opposite meanings? This proves the fact that it is possible to change and still be the same. Both of these words appear in Scripture. The *first* word appears in the above quoted passage of Romans 12:2, where it says, "Be transformed." The *second* word appears in 2 Corinthians 11:13–15 (NIV). See if you can pick it out:

> For such men are false apostles, deceitful workmen, masquerading as apostles of Christ. And no wonder, for satan himself masquerades as an angel of light. It is not surprising, then, if his servants masquerade as servants of righteousness. Their end will be what their actions deserve.

Did you find it? It actually appears three times in three different forms in the text! The root word is *masquerade* (which is a fancy word for putting on a mask or disguise). This verse basically says that even as satan himself masquerades/disguises as an angel of light, so there are many people on this earth who disguise themselves. They like to look good on the outside, but they have not dealt with changing their hearts on the inside. In reality, they have only changed their outward appearance, without changing the motives of their hearts.

As believers we like to talk the talk, but can we walk the walk? We talk about wanting to live for God, but when it comes down to it, we can fall into the tendency to just put on a mask. We act like we have it all together and like we're good, but where are our hearts? If we have not allowed God to come and transform our hearts, then all we are doing is wearing a mask.

Many people may speak of transformation. They may say they long for true revival. But they are not willing to undergo true transformation themselves. The challenge for us is to not be like this. There is a price that comes with true change and transformation. Many are not willing to pay it, for it can be a painful process to allow the Lord to transform our hearts, especially if there is a lot of junk in there that He needs to strip out. But we are called to count the costs. If we want transformation or revival in our churches, our schools, our cities, or our families, we must first be willing to examine our own hearts to see if there is any personal transformation needed. Transforming revival in a nation, a city, a church, or a school has to begin with transforming revival in individual people's hearts.

With this in mind, we have a choice to make: Will we simply wear a mask and pretend to serve God or will we allow Him to truly transform us? May this be our heart's cry: Transform us, Lord. Transform us. Don't let us put on our masks and disguises any longer. We don't want to just go through the motions; we want to truly live for you. We don't want to pretend to serve You with our lips if our hearts are far from you. Transform us from the inside out. Start with our hearts. Don't let us be externally changed without being internally changed. Simply transform us every day, so that we may become more like You. Transform us, Lord. Transform us.

Day 21:
He Wants It All

The more I have grown and learned about worship, the more I have realized that worship is way more than the songs we sing and the hands we raise. The biggest indicator of our worship to God is not found in a multitude of words, songs, or postures. Rather, the biggest indicator of our worship comes from a life of obedience to His Word.

First John 5:3 (NIV) tells us, "This is love for God: to keep His commands." If we sing about our love for God but intentionally live in disobedience, our words are empty. We worship God by obeying Him. We obey Him by obeying His Word and those He has placed in authority over us. For this reason, we can see that worship is more than just singing. Worship is a lifestyle.

Colossians 3:23 (NIV) tells us, "Whatever you do, work at it with all your heart, as working for the Lord, not for human masters, since you know that you will receive an inheritance from the Lord as a reward. It is the Lord Christ you are serving." We worship God in everything we do! Thus, our singing should be an outflow of a life of worship! We must not talk the talk if we are not willing to walk the walk. I believe the Lord takes this very seriously.

In Amos 5:23 (NIV), the Lord said, "Away with the noise of your songs! I will not listen to the music of your harps." He said this because the people were praising God with their lips, yet their hearts were far from Him. You see, songs sung to God out of impure hearts are just a bunch of noise: noise that God refuses to listen to. But making a joyful noise in obedience—now *that* is clearly joyful worship. What good is it to sing these songs if we don't really mean it? What good is it to raise our hands if we aren't taking time with God seriously?

Jesus addressed the Pharisees on this issue as well. He said, "Woe to you, teachers of the law and Pharisees, you hypocrites! You are like whitewashed tombs, which look beautiful on the outside but on the inside are full of the bones of the dead and everything unclean. In the same way, on the outside you appear to people as righteous but on the inside you are full of hypocrisy and wickedness" (Matthew 23:27–28, NIV). My concern is that it has become way too easy for us to fall into the same trap as the religious leaders of Jesus' day. We have become really good at making ourselves look good on the outside. But God sees our hearts.

What sins are we intentionally holding on to that are hindering the effectiveness of our worship? I'm not talking about the occasional sin or mistake. I'm talking about ongoing, habitual sin that we really have no intention of changing. How can we say we worship God when we're living like the world? What are our motives? Where are our hearts? God wants ALL of me. He wants ALL of you. He doesn't just want our songs; He wants our lives. Will we give that to Him?

Day 22: Lord *and* Savior

Many times when people ask Jesus into their hearts and put their faith in Him, they pray a prayer that includes a phrase that goes something like this: "Jesus, please be my Lord and Savior." However, I have a concern that many who have prayed this prayer do not fully understand what this phrase means. If Jesus is to be our Lord *and* our Savior, then we need to make sure we understand what both of those things really mean.

Let's start with the easier one: Savior. The word *Savior* deals with our eternal destiny. We love this word. After all, one of the big reasons we come to Jesus is that we recognize that we are dead in our sins, and we need a Savior to rescue us from eternal spiritual death. It is because of Jesus our Savior that we can have eternal life. Jesus died on the cross, rose from the dead on the third day, and conquered sin, death, and the grave for our sakes. It is because of His atoning sacrifice for us on the cross that we can now experience His powerful grace and forgiveness. We can experience eternal life with Jesus because He is our Savior.

But now let's look at the more difficult word: Lord. The word *Lord* deals with the discipleship process here on earth, and it is a costly word. No, it might not literally cost us money, but it signifies the cost of being a disciple of

Christ. This is not a word that we like as much. No, this word comes with a price, and not everyone is willing to pay that price. You see, *Savior* has to do with the price that Jesus paid for us, but *Lord* has to do with the cost of living for Him.

For Jesus to be Lord of our lives, it means that He is given complete control. We give up our rights to drive our lives. We get out of the driver's seat and let Him take over. The first definition of the word *Lord* in the dictionary is: "Someone or something having power, authority, or influence; a master or ruler." This definition creates a problem for those people who want to be in control and run their own lives. And if we're honest, we are all at least somewhat control freaks, right? It's hard for us to give up control! We have this tendency to want to manage everything in our lives—but that's a huge problem, because when we do that, we leave no room for Jesus. We only want Jesus in our lives on our terms and when it's convenient.

We love to make Jesus our Savior, but we don't always love to make Him Lord—because when He is Lord, we have to give Him full control. When He is Lord, we might have to follow Him even if our families and friends reject us. When He is Lord, we might need to obey Him even when He tells us to do something that is way outside our comfort zones. When He is Lord, we might face all kinds of ridicule and persecution because of our determination to stand up for what's right. And when He is Lord, it requires that we ultimately put our old selves to death.

The Bible says that we are not our own, but we were bought with a price (1 Cor. 6:19–20). That means that when we give our lives to Jesus, we can't just call Him our Savior without serving Him as our Lord. It means that He actually owns us now. However, we don't serve and love Him because we have to, but because we want to. When Jesus is our Lord and Savior, our natural response is that our hearts will fall madly in love with Him, and we will want to live for Him with everything we have. With this in mind, Jesus, we make this our prayer: Come be our Lord *and* Savior. Come do what You want to do in us and with us and through us. We give it all to You—everything. Come and change our lives for Your glory, Saving Lord. Amen.

Day 23:
Get Hungry

One of the biggest deterrents to hunger is satisfaction. When we feel satisfied, we no longer feel the need to eat. It is when we are unsatisfied that we keep eating. Of course, there is a spiritual application to this.

You see, the world and its pleasures are like candy. We can eat a lot of candy and feel "satisfied," for we become so full of sugary substances that we don't want to eat anything else. We feel full, and we may think we're satisfied, yet we have eaten nothing of substance—nothing of lasting value. After all, you know what your parents used to tell you: "Don't eat that candy before your meal. You'll spoil your dinner!"

In the same way, the more we eat of the candy this world has to offer, the more it steals our appetites from the things of God. The candy of this world gives us the false feeling of satisfaction, when all that it really leaves us with is nutrition deficiency and a stomachache. We misinterpret this stomachache as meaning that we ate too much; however, that is only partially true.

The reality is that we ate too much of the wrong thing, but not nearly enough of the right thing. Sometimes, we are so sick to our stomach with the things of the world, that we can't imagine being hungry for anything. It is at those times that we must actually purge ourselves of the worldly foods we've been eating because those foods have become like poison to us. Much like our bodies respond to food poisoning by purging everything out, so we must purge ourselves of the things of the world. The process is not pleasant, but afterwards, we will find ourselves healthy and hungry once again, filled with a desire for real food: the Word, presence, and power of God.

So how do we purge ourselves? We can start by simply asking God to increase our hunger for Him. I believe He loves to respond to that prayer, but we need to be ready for the process He might lead us through. The spiritual purging process requires a death to self—it requires us bowing to the Lord's will and becoming willing to do whatever it takes to get our hunger back. The Scriptures put it this way: "I am the LORD your God, Who brought you out of the land of Egypt; Open your mouth wide, and I will fill it" (Psa. 81:10). Also, "Blessed are those who hunger and thirst for righteousness, for they shall be filled" (Matt. 5:6).

So the question remains: Will you do it? Will I do it? Will we do whatever it takes to grow in our hunger for God? Or will we stay contented to live on the food of the world, which gives the appearance of satisfaction but carries no substance? The choice is ours. I don't know about you, but I'm asking God to increase my hunger for Him, no matter what the cost may be. Let's get hungry again.

Day 24:
The Pressure Is OFF: No More Striving

If we stop to think about it, I believe we would be surprised to realize just how much of our lives revolve around performance. I know that, for me, my whole life could become a performance if I'm not careful. At work, I am a teacher, so I can all too easily find myself in a place of "performing," both for my students and those in authority, always trying to perfect my skills and techniques. At church, I am a music minister and teacher of the Bible—frequently in the frontlines, and often in a position where a performance could be the natural outcome. Then there's my personal life, in which you might think that I would just let down my hair and relax. Yet, even at these times, I find a performance mindset try to creep in, trying to put on some kind of performance for my family and friends.

To top that all off, one of my greatest strengths is that I am an achiever; yet, this strength has a tendency to overpower itself and morph into a perfectionist mindset if I'm not careful. I can do these things in the name of excellence, which is a great goal in and of itself. I believe the Lord does call us to excellence. However, before I know it, what I define as excellence can become an obsession—a burden I was never meant to carry.

The biggest danger of a performance mindset is that it compels us to measure our worth by our achievements. Thus, to feel valued and worthy, we have to be constantly performing and achieving the next thing. If we don't meet expectations, we don't feel valued or loved. Well, here's a news flash: People's expectations of are often unrealistic and higher than we can ever hope to achieve. If we live a life that revolves around performing for people, we will ultimately fail at trying to meet everyone's expectations. We can't always please people. At some point, we will let them down because either (a) we make a mistake or (b) their expectations of us are unrealistically high and totally unattainable.

But here is the good news: We were never meant to live this way. God didn't make us for performance; He made us for relationship. When He created man, He didn't want someone to put on a show for Him; He wanted someone who would walk in deep connection and relationship with Him. I have heard it said that we were not made for perfection; we were made for connection.

About a year ago, I remember taking some time to listen to the Lord, and I sensed Him so clearly speak to my spirit: "The pressure is OFF." He spoke this to me at a time when I was heavily relying on my performance to get me through that season of life. Yet, what He spoke to me so clearly was that my performance would fail me sooner or later. I needed to stop building my foundation on a performance and instead build it on His love, because His love never fails. True love *never* involves striving. The more we strive for love, the more we deny ourselves the very freedom that love brings.

God is calling us to a place of less "doing" and more "being." If our worth is based on what we do, we will find that we can never do enough. We have to realize that our worth is not based on what we do but who we are. We are children of God. He loves us because of who we are. He values us because of who we are. Our achievements may seem significant in the eyes of man, but soon those achievements will only fade and have to be replaced by more achievements. The Lord does not look at what man looks at, for man looks at the external factors, but the Lord looks at the heart (1 Sam. 16:7). As He looks at our hearts, may He not find a mindset of striving for perfection; rather, may He find true love for Him and for other people. That kind of love is what the Scripture tells us will never fail (1 Cor. 13:8). After all, we can never find excellence apart from the pursuit of love, for love is the "more excellent way" (1 Cor. 12:31).

Let's agree to cease our striving. This only leads to exhaustion and burnout. Let's agree instead to be ever on a journey of learning more about how to love and how to live in connection with our Lord and Savior, Who loves us for who we are, not for what we have or haven't done. As we do this, we will surely find that the pressure is off.

Day 25:
The Praise of God

"Nevertheless even among the rulers many believed in [Jesus], but because of the Pharisees they did not confess Him, lest they should be put out of the synagogue; for they loved the praise of men more than the praise of God."

~John 12:42–43

Peer pressure. As much as we'd like to say it's not a real thing and pretend it doesn't exist, we know that it is actually a very powerful force. Adults have a tendency to brush it off and say, "Oh, peer pressure is only something that affects children. I'm an adult now, and I don't care what other people think of me." Anyone who says that is either in denial or a liar. Peer pressure doesn't go away when we get older; it is the same beast, but with a different mask. To some degree, we all care about what other people think of us. We all have something in us that seeks after the praise of men.

Psychology even supports this claim. Studies have shown that we are creatures of conformity. We will tend to act or behave in a way that conforms to the group we are in. We will dress like them, eat like them, talk like them, and act like them. Why? Because if we don't do what we see everyone else doing, we are concerned that they will think of us as "weird." We don't want to be different. We don't want to be weird. We want to be normal. We want to fit in. So we live our entire lives striving to meet some self-imposed standard, some imagined expectation that we must fit in.

Now, peer pressure isn't always a bad thing; in fact, sometimes it can be very good. It is not wrong to seek affirmation or approval from other people. But when that becomes our main focus, then we have lost the joy of living. Why do we seek so hard after the approval of other people? I think it is because we have lost sight of Whose approval really matters. You see, the Scripture passage from John 12 listed at the top of this devotion tells us that there were people in Jesus' days who wanted to believe in Him and follow Him, but they were afraid of what would happen to them if they did. They cared more about what other people thought of them than what God thought of them. It is not wrong for us to love the "praise of men," as the Scripture calls it; but when we love the praise of men more than the praise of God, then we have a serious problem. If we don't live our lives to please God first, then we have just allowed man's approval to take first place in our lives and actually become an idol.

The Lord tells us this in His Word: "Do not be conformed to this world, but be transformed by the renewing of your mind, that you may prove what is that good and acceptable and perfect will of God" (Rom. 12:2). To *conform* means to adjust to one's surroundings or to become like something. When we try to act a certain way just to get other people to like us or approve of us, we are conforming. But have we forgotten that we're not supposed to look like the world? God's Word has another option: Instead of being *conformed*, we are to be *transformed*. We are to be changed into the people God has created us to be! As Christians, we are not called to blend in. We are called to stand out—to be light in this dark world. If we keep acting like everyone around us, we are only adding darkness to darkness. It's hard to be a light, but it's the only thing that will make a difference in this dark world. So make this your challenge: Be a light today. Don't be afraid to stand out. Jesus dared to be different, and so should we. Seek God's approval today.

Day 26:
My Life as a Game of Whac-A-Mole

Have you ever played the classic arcade game called Whac-A-Mole? It's the game where you are given a hammer and a time limit, and every time a plastic mole pops out of one of several holes in the machine, you have to whack it back down. The more moles you whack down within the given time limit, the higher your score will be.

Do you ever feel like your life is like that game? No matter how desperately hard you try to whack all the moles down and keep them down, another one inevitably comes up. I liken it to one person trying to keep multiple stringless helium balloons from rising at the same time or to someone trying to herd ten cats and get them all to go to the same place at the same time. It's exhausting and next to impossible.

But this is all too often a picture of our lives.

I have to make a confession: Apart from the Spirit of God, I am a natural control freak. And I don't think I'm alone. As humans, we strive so hard to keep everything under control in our lives. We want the perfect job, the perfect salary, the perfect house, the perfect car, the perfect spouse, and the perfect family. We fight so desperately hard to maintain our image so that others think that we've got everything under control. However, in reality, we are secretly exhausting ourselves while losing a daily battle to maintain control. The further we go in life, the faster the moles keep appearing, and the harder it is to maintain control. Pretty soon, the secret can no longer be a secret. The moles get loose. Chaos erupts. And all the onlookers realize that our lives are not as under control as they thought they were.

Sometimes we spend years creating an image of ourselves intended to impress everyone around us. We build ourselves a kingdom, name ourselves the king, and begin to compete against other kingdoms. But we can only keep up the façade for so long before it all comes crashing down.

All the moles pop up at once.

All the helium balloons escape our grasp.

All ten cats go in ten different directions.

And we are left with nothing to show for it.

When we get to this point, we become broken—painfully broken. We feel like we have completely lost control. For some people, it's losing a job. For others, it's losing money. Still others find they have lost a loved one through death or that they've lost their marriage to divorce. There are those who developed a life-threatening disease. Some lose a home to foreclosure or to a natural disaster. And there are even those whose secret sin becomes publicly exposed. For others, it is perhaps not quite so intense, yet still very significant—maybe it's getting kicked off a team, breaking up with a girlfriend, or failing a class. But whatever the circumstances may be, they all ultimately lead us back to the same place—a place of brokenness and a loss of control.

And that's exactly where God wants us.

No, I am not saying God likes to see us suffer. But He does love to see us surrender. It would be far easier if we just gave the hammer to God and let Him take care of the moles from the start. But far too often, our human pride says, "It's ok, God, I've got this." At the beginner's level of the game, that might be true; but what happens when it gets to the expert level? All of a sudden, we can't keep up. It's easy to think we have life under control when everything is easy and going well in life. But what happens when things start falling apart? Where do we go then? If we've truly given the control to God, then we will be safe and secure in the midst of the chaos. But if we try to keep the control for ourselves, we will quickly become exhausted, burn ourselves out, and fail.

The main point is this: No matter how hard we try to control our lives, there are things that will happen that we have absolutely no control over. I believe that Jesus is speaking a message to us loud and clear: "Give me your keys," He says. "Let me take care of all the moles. Let me do it in the way that only I can. Let me truly have control of your life so that I can use you for My glory."

Christians often say that we've given God control; yet for many, it's just a saying that sounds good but contains no meaning. There's no doubt that we love Jesus and want to serve Him, but we want it all on our terms and in our controlled environment. The problem is: God doesn't work in a controlled environment. Actually, He thrives on working through chaos and confusion to establish His Kingdom order. It's how He created the world. And it's how He wants to work in our lives too.

So give Him your mess today. Everything that you've been holding so tightly for so long, just release it all to Him now. Feel the weight lift off your shoulders as you do that. You were never meant to be in control. And you aren't very good at it.

Why not let Him take it from here?

Day 27:
So, You Think You're Entitled?

Recently, I invited myself to a party. It was a pretty lame party. I was the only guest on the list. After all, no one wants to attend your own pity party. But let's back up. How and why did this happen?

Well, a variety of factors led up to it, but it was primarily connected to a busy schedule and a full plate of things to do. And through all this, I became stressed and began to think I deserved something or another for all my trouble. The more I mulled this over in my mind, the more I began to feel entitled to certain things. Suddenly, it seemed that the whole world became indebted to me.

Thankfully, Someone came in and crashed my party—and that Someone was God. He lovingly but firmly chided me, saying, "So, you think you're entitled, huh?"

I didn't want to listen. But He kept at it.

He continued, "I sent My Son for you. He threw away everything He deserved to take on the guilt, shame, suffering, and pain He did not deserve. So do you want to tell Me again *why* you think you're entitled?"

I didn't know what to say.

Then He took me to this verse: "You have been treated generously, so live generously" (Matt. 10:8, MSG). He showed me that He has called me to live a generous life because of the fullness of generosity He has already given me. "We love because He first loved us" (1 John 4:19, NIV). We serve because He first served us. We give because He first gave to us.

We were entitled to nothing, yet He gave us everything. He didn't owe us anything, but He gave us His life. How can we respond in any way but with gratitude, thanksgiving, praise, generosity, and servitude? He doesn't force us to serve Him out of obligation. But a life of sacrifice is our reasonable act of worship to Him (Rom. 12:1).

Okay, God, You got me. Forgive me for letting my selfishness get in the way of serving You. "Show me how to love like You have loved me."[xix] Amen.

Section VI:
Can I Get a Witness?

Day 28:
Only Light

As Christians, we have developed this all-too-cliché concept of how we just need to shine the light of Jesus everywhere. But, as cliché as it is, it actually carries an enormous amount of weight. The problem is that we have become so used to saying it that the phrase has somehow lost some of its impact along the way.

Let me keep this short and sweet and share something that just might put a little extra spark back into this phrase. For some people, *you might be the only light they see* throughout their day. Think about that. People who don't have Jesus in their lives are in state of perpetual darkness. Jesus explained them as being harassed, helpless, and like sheep without a shepherd (Matt. 9:36). So that coworker you just can't stand; that angry person in line at the store; that acquaintance who always seems to push your buttons; that family member who just rubs you the wrong way—for all these and more, have you ever thought that they actually might be attracted to you because of the light that you carry? They might not ever show it or admit it—in fact, they might even seem to act toward the contrary of it—but maybe, just maybe there is something about you that intrigues them. A person who is used to living in utter darkness might simultaneously be repulsed, while also fascinated, and drawn in by a sudden appearance of light—thus, that person will be conflicted with how to respond.

So what is our job? Our job is to keep shining. God has given us a light, and for some people, it is the only light they may have ever seen—and it is the very light that will lead them to the cross. Don't underestimate the power of the light that you carry. Don't try to hide it and drive the people away. Keep shining. Shine brightly. Let everyone know that darkness is not their only option. There is a Light that drives out the darkness. There is a Love that casts out every fear. And His name is Jesus. And He lives and shines through you and me.

Day 29: The Power of the Holy Spirit

When people think about the Holy Spirit, they can sometimes become uneasy or uncomfortable. This is because we tend to think of the Holy Spirit as weird or spooky or something mysterious that we shouldn't dare get too close to. Of course, these feelings and fears are understandable; however, they are not founded in Scripture. The Holy Spirit is not spooky or scary. He is not some sort of mystical or magical force. He is not simply an "it" or an object. He is not some make-believe imaginary friend. No, the Holy Spirit is none of these things.

The Holy Spirit is God. The Holy Spirit is a Person—one of three members of the Trinity. Our God, Yahweh, is one God in three Persons: Father, Son (Jesus), and Holy Spirit. Nothing can stop Him; nothing can overcome Him; and nothing can overpower Him. Yet, it is amazing how many believers in God are so unwilling to talk about or acknowledge the power of the Holy Spirit. They will freely talk about God the Father and God the Son, but when it comes to God the Holy Spirit, they will keep quiet. Why is this? What is it that keeps us back from allowing the Holy Spirit to work His power in our lives? Oftentimes, it is our own fears, misperceptions, or even ignorance that hinder the Spirit from moving.

The Holy Spirit longs to work in us and through us. We have often heard that, when we committed our lives to the Lord and asked Him to save us from our sins, Jesus then came to live in our hearts. But do we realize that at that time the Holy Spirit also came to dwell in us? First Corinthians 3:16 asks this question: "Do you not know that you are the temple of God and that the Spirit of God dwells in you?" For those of us who are believers, we already have the Holy Spirit in us! Yet, not all of us walk in the Spirit. We do not always operate in the fullness of the Spirit. To me, the above verse implies that it is possible to have the Spirit dwelling in us and yet not recognize or acknowledge His presence and power in our lives. That is a very sobering thought.

With this in mind, the Scripture also declares: "Do not grieve the Holy Spirit of God, by whom you were sealed for the day of redemption" (Eph. 4:30). I think that we grieve the Holy Spirit when we do not acknowledge His fullness in our lives. I think we grieve Him when we deny His power in our lives and try to live by our own strength instead. And I think we grieve Him when we do not walk in the Spirit but instead tune out His voice and determine to live according to our own ways.

We need to realize that the Spirit of Him Who raised Christ from the dead also lives in us and gives us power to walk daily with Him! Romans 8:11 tells us, "But if the Spirit of Him who raised Jesus from the dead dwells in you, He who raised Christ from the dead will also give life to your mortal bodies through His Spirit who dwells in you." The Holy Spirit empowers us to do His work! Why would we want to resist that power and walk around trying to accomplish anything with our own strength? We need His power. We need His presence in our lives!

It was by the power of the Holy Spirit that Peter preached to a multitude of people, and thousands of people were added to the Church in one day. It was by the power of the Holy Spirit that different people spoke the gospel message in many languages at once, which led thousands of people to repentance. It was by the power of the Holy Spirit that Peter and John brought healing to a crippled man at the temple gate. It was by the power of the Holy Spirit that Philip was teleported from one place to another so he could preach the gospel to a specific person. It was by the power of the Holy Spirit that Peter's chains fell off him in prison and he was set free to continue to preach the gospel.

And it is the same power from the same Holy Spirit that dwells in you and me today. But we can't deny Him, quench Him, or grieve Him; we must learn to daily walk in the power of the Spirit!

The Holy Spirit wasn't just given to the people in the book of Acts. The Holy Spirit wasn't just someone who existed in Bible times but isn't necessary anymore. No, the Holy Spirit is real. The Holy Spirit is powerful. He is just as real and powerful today as He ever was.

With that in mind, just think about how He might want to work in your life today. He is the God of miracles. He is the God of salvation. He is the God of redemption. And He is the God of resurrection. He wants to empower you so that you are immersed in His presence. He didn't intend for you to walk the Christian walk without having His power live in you. So open up your heart to Him. Invite Him to work in a new way in your life today. Welcome Him in all of His fullness. I assure you that, if you do, you will never be the same—and God will be glorified in you!

Day 30:
Take a Stand

> *"Blessed are those who are persecuted because of righteousness, for theirs is the kingdom of heaven. Blessed are you when people insult you, persecute you and falsely say all kinds of evil against you because of Me. Rejoice and be glad, because great is your reward in heaven."*
> ~Matthew 5:10–12 (NIV)

You don't have to be a Christian for very long before you realize that not everyone will like the fact that You live for Jesus. By following Jesus, we make a specific choice to go against the ways of the world we live in. We will find ourselves having to make difficult decisions to take a stand for Christ in the midst of a sinful world. When we do this and take a stand for Christ, we can expect that opposition will come. There really is no question about it.

The only question is not about *whether* it will come, but about *how* it will come. For some, persecution surfaces in the form of physical abuse, imprisonment, slavery, torture, or even death. For others, there is no physical harm—but there is deep spiritual warfare and emotional pain from being accused, mocked, bullied, slandered, and cursed at. Regardless of how the persecution will come, we must ask ourselves this question: Are we willing to take a stand for

Christ, no matter what the consequences may be? Are we willing to lay it all on the line? Will we be on fire for God?

People will call us hateful because we stand for righteousness—but they don't realize that we're actually doing everything we can to show the love of Christ while still taking a stand for what's right. People will call us intolerant, judgmental, and critical just because we oppose the sin of the world and in the church. But do you know what our response must be? Joy and love.

We respond with joy because the Scripture tells us that we will receive an eternal reward because of the persecution we endure on this earth. Acts 5:41 tells us that when the apostles were persecuted they rejoiced "because they had been counted worthy of suffering disgrace for the Name" of Jesus. Imagine how dedicated the apostles must have been to actually be happy that they were worthy to suffer! *Worthy to suffer?* That's not something we talk about much; but maybe we need to start talking about it more. Oh, that we would respond with joy like the apostles did. Oh, that we would be counted worthy to suffer for Jesus' name.

We also respond with love, for love covers a multitude of sins (1 Pet. 4:8). Even though the world does not love us, we can still love this world with the love of Christ. How else will they hear the gospel? How else will they respond to His truth? In the midst of persecution, we must never lose our love. Just as Jesus loved a people who did not love Him, so we must show His love to everyone we encounter. Imagine what would happen if we did that! Lord, teach us how to take a stand for You—and teach us how to do it joyfully and with Your love.

Day 31: Compelled by Love

"...I consider my life worth nothing to me, if only I may finish the race and complete the task the Lord Jesus has given me–the task of testifying to the gospel of God's grace."
~Acts 20:24 (NIV)

"He said to them, 'Go into all the world and preach the gospel to all creation.'"
~Mark 16:15

God's command for us to go and preach His gospel message is a very familiar command that most believers are aware of. We know that we are supposed to go into all the world and preach the gospel. We know that God asks that we share His Word with people as often as we have the opportunity. Yet, for many of us, we view this more as an obligation—as something that we are simply expected to do. We add it to the list of rules that we must obey and requirements we must meet. And it is not necessarily wrong for us to do this; after all, it is a command of God to us.

But what if we viewed this from a different perspective? What if we viewed every opportunity to share God's Word as a privilege, rather than an obligation? That's what the Apostle Paul did. Paul went on multiple journeys, risking his life multiple times, all for the sake of preaching the gospel of Jesus Christ. Following a set of rules doesn't typically make anyone want to risk his or her life. If preaching the gospel is just an obligation, something we feel like we have to do, then we will have the tendency only to go so far—only to do the bare minimum. But what if there is something more?

What if we shared the gospel, not because we feel like we have to, but because we want to? What if we were so in love with Jesus that we just could not help speaking about what we have seen and heard (Acts 4:20)? The Apostle Paul was so passionate about preaching the good news of Jesus wherever he went that he said he considered his life nothing—he was willing to preach the gospel at any cost!

Think about it: Paul was beaten, mocked, and scorned. He was stoned and left for dead. He was imprisoned multiple times. He was taken as a prisoner, shipwrecked, and bitten by a poisonous snake. Yet, each time, the Lord spared him because the Lord still had more people who needed to hear the gospel. Paul didn't share the gospel because he felt like he had to. He shared the gospel because he wanted to— he was *compelled* to!

Second Corinthians 5:14 tells us that Christ's love compels us. This means that, when we are in Christ, we are so filled with His love that we cannot help but share it with everyone around us! So the question we must ask ourselves is: Are we compelled by Christ's love? Are we so passionately in love with Him that we will do whatever it takes to introduce others to Him as well?

As with so many other things, sharing the gospel really isn't about a list of rules and requirements. It's about a relationship—a deep, life-giving, fulfilling relationship with our Lord and Savior Jesus Christ, our Heavenly Father, and His Holy Spirit alive in us. Why would we not want to tell others about this amazing news? What are we afraid of? What are we waiting for? Let's let His love compel us to share His Word at every opportunity we have, trusting Him to speak through us in the ways that only He can!

Appendix A: Do You Know Him?

Dear friends,

The Word of God declares, "[Jesus is] the way, the truth, and the life. No one comes to the Father except through [Him]'" (John 14:6). I have written much about Jesus in this book, but I would be remiss to conclude this book without giving a special opportunity to you, the reader, to actually know Him and trust Him as your Lord and Savior. According to the verse above, Jesus is the *only* way to the Father; He is the only way by which men and women may receive eternal life.

You may ask, "What does that mean?" Well, some people call it "getting saved" or a "salvation experience." Others call it "giving your heart to Jesus" or "asking Jesus into your heart." All those terms are human attempts to describe the miracle that takes place when we, as fallen and sinful people, put our faith in Jesus Christ as the One Who saves us from the penalty of our sins: eternal torment and separation from God.

Unfortunately, many people overcomplicate salvation, declaring that people have to do x, y, and z in order to obtain or earn eternal life. However, the Bible is clear.

John 3:16 states it best: "For God so loved the world that He gave His only begotten Son, that whoever believes in Him should not perish but have everlasting life." If you want eternal life, you must simply believe (put your faith) in Jesus Christ: That He is Who He says He is (the Son of God, the second member of the Trinity), that He did what He said He did (came to earth as God in the flesh to die for the sins of the world and rose to life victoriously on the third day), and that He will do what He says He will do (return to take His church home with Him at the end of the age). Don't overcomplicate this. If you understand that you are a sinner in need of a Savior and believe that Jesus is your Lord and Savior, then I believe you are already saved at this moment. This is **justification**.

"But what about my lifestyle?" you may ask. "Surely, God demands some sort of good works in order for me to be saved." You are partially right. God commands us to be righteous and holy, but that follows as a result of salvation, not a requirement for salvation. This is called **sanctification**, and it is a cooperative work in which God and we participate together in the lifelong pursuit of holiness. In the natural, you don't become perfect immediately after putting your faith in Christ. Rather, the Lord starts you on a lifelong journey of learning how to live as He has called you to live, not according to the flesh, but according to the Spirit. However, the moment you put your faith in Christ, in God's eyes, you become holy. He makes you righteous, not because of what you have done, but because of what He has done.

Finally, at the end of our earthly lives, the Lord will take us home to live with Him eternally. This is **glorification**. Do you understand this message?

If you feel the nudging of the Lord to commit your life to Him, do it right now. Don't waste another minute without believing in Him. Pray and devote your life to Him. I want you to understand that your prayer is not what saves you; you are saved by grace and through faith, not through a token prayer. However, it is often helpful to mark your deciding moment with a prayer of dedication to God. With that in mind, I encourage you to pray a prayer in your own words to God right now. If you aren't sure what to say, I have even included an example prayer to help get you started. (But please don't simply ride on the back of my prayer. Personalize it for your own situation.)

> Jesus, I declare this day that I believe in You, that You are the Son of God, that You came to earth as a man, died for my sins, and rose again as the Victor over death. I repent of my sins and commit my life to You eternally. Please help me to live for You, and sanctify me according to Your truth. I am so excited to live eternally for You and with You!

If you made a conscious decision to believe in Jesus today and to live for Him eternally, I am absolutely ecstatic for you! It is the best and most important decision of your life. Please do me a favor. Email me at runningfree@cox.net if you made this decision. Ask me if you have any further questions as well. Get into a good Bible-believing church if you aren't already attending one and surround yourself with other believers. Keep reading your Bible and developing your prayer life every day. This is not a checklist of things to do, but all these things will help you in your Christian walk and your sanctification process.

If you did not yet make a decision but would like more information, please email me at the above address too. I would love to chat with you and help in any way I can.

For His cause,

Jason B. West

runningfree@cox.net

Appendix B: Other Products Available from Anointed 2 Go MdM

Books

Downloads from Heaven

Instructions and Examples of Hearing from God

By Jay W. West

Suggested donation: $10

Kingdom Encounters

Keys to Unlocking God's Treasures

By Jay W. West and Jason B. West

Suggested donation: $12

Well Well Well

By Jay W. West

Suggested donation: $12

Who Will Ascend?

Taking Prayer to Another Level

By Jason B. West

Suggested donation: $10

Willing to Yield

Discover How "Yielding" Accesses the Supernatural Wisdom, Favor, and Power of God

By Jay W. West

Suggested donation: $10

Music CD

Running Free

Original songs by Jason B. West

Suggested donation: $10

*Also available on iTunes and www.cdbaby.com

To order these and other products from Anointed 2 Go, please contact:

Jason West at runningfree@cox.net

www.kingdomexpressions.wordpress.com

Or

Jay West at anointed2go@cox.net

www.kingdomencounters.net

Please note that minimal shipping costs will be added to each order, which vary slightly with each order.

Appendix C
Notes

---

i. Luke 17:5

ii. "Hosanna" by Brooke Fraser. © 2006 Hillsong Publishing.

iii. Adapted from 1 Corinthians 13:4–8 (NIV)

iv. "Good Good Father" by Anthony Brown and Pat Barrett. © 2014 Pat Barrett Music (Admin. by Joseph Barrett).

v. "No Longer Slaves" by Jonathan David Helser and Melissa Helser. © 2014 Bethel Music Publishing.

vi. Continue reading for a personal illustration of this in Day 6.

vii. See Genesis 18.

viii. See Exodus 32.

ix. See John 2.

x. Luke 17:5

xi. Romans 8:11

xii. "Here as in Heaven" by Chris Brown, Mack Brock, Matthew Ntlele, Steven Furtick, and Wade Joye. © 2015 Music by Elevation Worship Publishing

(Admin. by Essential Music Publishing LLC).

[xiii]. See Days 7 & 8 about Faith.

[xiv]. See John 2.

[xv]. See Exodus 32.

[xvi]. See Isaiah 38.

[xvii]. Matthew 7:7 (AMP)

[xviii] Pastors Duaine and Latosha Johnson pastor Purpose Church in St. Louis, Missouri.

[xix]. "Hosanna" by Brooke Fraser. © 2006 Hillsong Publishing.

www.ingramcontent.com/pod-product-compliance
Lightning Source LLC
Chambersburg PA
CBHW052052070526
44584CB00017B/2144